QUILTING FOR BUSY BOOMERS™

Edited by Jeanne Stauffer & Sandra L. Hatch

HOUSE of
WHITE
BIRCHES
PUBLISHERS
SINCE 1947

QUILTING FOR BUSY BOOMERS™

Editors: Jeanne Stauffer, Sandra L. Hatch

Art Director: Brad Snow

Publishing Services Director: Brenda Gallmeyer

Managing Editor: Dianne Schmidt

Assistant Art Director: Nick Pierce

Copy Supervisor: Michelle Beck

Copy Editors: Nicki Lehman, Mary O'Donnell

Technical Artist: Connie Rand

Graphic Arts Supervisor: Ronda Bechinski

Graphic Artist: Amy S. Lin

Production Assistants: Marj Morgan, Judy Neuenschwander

Photography Supervisor: Tammy Christian

Photography: Don Clark, Matthew Owen

Photo Stylist: Tammy Steiner

Printed in the USA

First Printing in China: 2008

Library of Congress Control Number: 2007926093

Hardcover ISBN: 978-1-59217-192-7

Softcover ISBN: 978-1-59217-199-6

DRGbooks.com

3 4 5 6 7 8 9

WELCOME

We live in an age when everyone is too busy. Slow down a little and take time out of your crazy life to enjoy yourself. Take time to quilt. You can relax and be productive at the same time! Not only will your loved ones enjoy the fruits of your labor, they will notice how refreshed you are after making time to do something you enjoy.

Learning new skills can be a lot of fun. If you are just starting to quilt, you are in for so much fun! Don't worry about everything being just right. Enjoy what you are doing, and your skills will develop rapidly. If you are an experienced quilter, learn a new quilting technique; relax and enjoy yourself as you increase your knowledge of quilting. With every project, you have the opportunity to buy more fabric or a new tool to try. Whatever project you select to make, we give you drawings or photos to explain each step of the way. The wonderful thing about quilting is that your work doesn't need to be perfect. If it looks good to you, it is good.

If you want to enjoy your quilting even more, find a friend who needs a relaxing hobby. Together you will stitch and stitch, relaxing with each loving stitch that you make. Quilting is a time of fun and adventure. All you need to do is select a pattern, and you're on your way.

Jeanne Stauffer

Sandra L. Hatch

TABLE OF CONTENTS

Unbelievably Easy Quilts That Anyone Can Make

10 The Scent of Lilacs

13 Fancy Bars

16 Almost Amish Scrap Quilt

19 Scrappy Four Patch

22 Red, White & Blue Americana

Never Thought You'd See a Quilt Here

25 Fancy Needlework Basket

28 Quilted Fridge Frames

33 All-Sports Growth Chart

38 Trailing Ivy Roll Cover

41 Trailing Ivy Tissue Box Cover

Appliqué Quilts Add a Whole New Dimension

47 Posie Party

50 Pretty in Pink

53 Ducks in a Row

56 Rooster Wall Quilt

60 Stained Glass Circles

64 Sunflower Table Runner

67 Ladybug Runner

There's More Than One Way to Cut a Quilt

71 20/20 Spring Fling

74 Blooming Flowers

78 Toy Boat Regatta

86 Cookie-Cutter Crazy

The Only Thing Better Than a Quilt Is a Quilt With Accessories

90 Patchwork Posies

96 Dainty Handkerchief

99 A Touch of Elegance

Pieced Quilts Are Still the Favorite of Many

116 Springtime Table Mat

119 Table Grace

122 Fourth of July Picnic Blanket

125 Field of Sunflowers

128 Picture This

131 Happy Days

134 Square Dance

137 Strips & Stripes

140 Four-Square Fantasy

Quilting for Christmas Makes the Holiday Extra Special

145 Merry Christmas Bag

148 Happy Snowmen
    Place Mat

154 Christmas Holly
    Place Mat

157 Beaded Patchwork
    Ornaments

162 Shimmering
    Snowflakes

167 Twinkle, Twinkle
    Christmas Stars

How-to Material

7   Quiltmaking Basics

45 Special Appliqué
    Techniques

110 Special Piecing
    Techniques

170 Finishing Instructions

176 Special Thanks

176 Fabrics & Supplies

UNBELIEVABLY EASY QUILTS THAT ANYONE CAN MAKE

You've been busy with your family, busy working and now you have time to do something you've wanted to do for a long time: QUILT! Here are basic instructions and projects to get you started. If you're ready for more of a challenge, look ahead at the other chapters.

QUILTMAKING BASICS

MATERIALS & SUPPLIES

FABRICS

Use 100 percent cotton fabrics.

THREAD

Use good-quality cotton or cotton-covered polyester.

BATTING

Batting gives a quilt loft or thickness. It also adds warmth. Purchase the size large enough to cut the size you need for your quilt.

TOOLS & EQUIPMENT

There are few truly essential tools and little equipment required for quilt making. Basics include needles (start with size 9 and adjust as you become more experienced), pins (long, thin, sharp pins are best), scissors, a thimble, template materials (plastic or cardboard), marking tools (chalk marker, water-erasable pen or a No. 2 pencil), a rotary cutter, cutting mat and ruler, and a quilting frame or hoop.

CONSTRUCTION METHODS

CUTTING

Quick Cutting. Many pieces for quilts can be cut using a rotary cutter with a plastic ruler and mat. To prepare fabric for quick cutting, follow the steps below.

1. Straighten raw edges of fabric by folding fabric in fourths across the width as shown in Figure 1.

2. Press down flat; place ruler on fabric square with edge of fabric and make one cut from the folded

edge to the outside edge. If strips are not straightened, a wavy strip will result as shown in Figure 2. Always cut away from your body, holding the ruler firmly with the non-cutting hand.

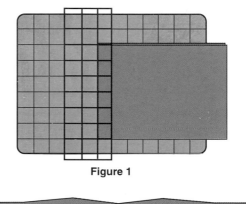

Figure 1

Figure 2

3. Follow the instructions given with each pattern for the size and number of cuts to make.

Traditional Templates. There are two types of templates that include a ¼" seam allowance (see Machine Piecing on page 8) and those that don't. For hand piecing and appliqué, use instructions below to cut out templates without seam allowances.

1. Place the template on the wrong side of the fabric.

2. Trace around shape.

3. Move template, leaving ½" between the shapes and mark again.

4. Cut out pieces, leaving ¼" beyond marked line all around each piece.

PIECING

Hand Piecing. When joining two pieces by hand, it is easier to begin with templates that do not include the ¼" seam allowance. For accurate piecing, follow the instructions below.

1. To join two units, place the patches with right sides together.

Figure 3

2. Stick a pin in at the beginning of the seam through both fabric patches, matching the beginning points (Figure 3); the seam begins on the traced line, not at the edge of the fabric (see Figure 4).

Figure 4

3. Thread a sharp needle; knot one strand of the thread at the end. Remove the pin and insert the needle in the hole; make a short stitch and then a backstitch right over the first stitch.

4. Continue making short stitches with several stitches on the needle at one time. As you stitch, check the back piece often.

5. Take a stitch at the end of the seam; backstitch and knot at the same time as shown in Figure 5.

Machine Piecing. Include the ¼" seam allowance on the template for machine piecing.

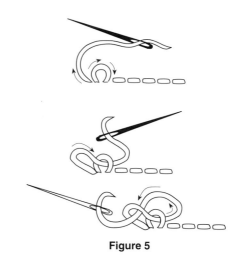

Figure 5

1. Place template on the wrong side of the fabric

2. Trace around shape.

3. Move template, butting pieces against one another.

4. Cut out pieces

Set machine on 2.5 or 12–15 stitches per inch. Join pieces as for hand piecing, beginning and ending sewing at the end of the fabric patch. No backstitching is necessary when machine-stitching.

APPLIQUÉ

Making Templates. Using a light box, transfer design to fabric background.

If you don't have a light box, tape the pattern on a window; center the background block on top and tape in place. Trace the design onto the background block with a No. 2 pencil. This drawing marks where the fabric pieces should be placed.

Hand Appliqué. Traditional hand appliqué uses a template made from the desired finished shape without seam allowance added.

1. Trace the desired shape onto the right side of the

fabric with marking tool. Leave at least ½" between design motifs when tracing to allow for the seam allowance when cutting out the shapes.

2. When the desired number of shapes needed has been drawn on the fabric pieces, cut out shapes leaving ⅛"–¼" all around drawn line for turning under.

3. Finger-press the shape's edges over on the drawn line. When turning in concave curves, clip to seams and baste the seam allowance over as shown in Figure 6.

Figure 6

4. Position the fabric shapes on the background block and pin them in place.

5. Using a blind stitch, sew pieces in place with matching thread and small stitches. Start with background pieces first and work up to foreground pieces.

Machine Appliqué. Fusible transfer web makes the machine-appliqué process easier. It is similar to iron-on interfacing except it has two sticky sides. Using an iron, follow the instructions below to adhere the appliqué shapes to the background block.

1. Reverse pattern and draw shapes onto the paper side of the fusible web.

2. Cut, leaving a margin around each shape.

3. Place on the wrong side of the chosen fabric; fuse in place referring to the manufacturer's instructions.

4. Cut out shapes on the drawn line.

5. Peel off the paper and fuse in place on the background fabric. Transfer any detail lines to the fabric shapes. ■

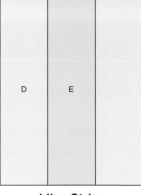

Lilac Stripe
4½" x 6" Block
Make 24

THE SCENT OF LILACS

Design by Connie Kauffman

You can almost smell the lilacs in bloom on this pretty quilt made with lilac prints.

PROJECT SPECIFICATIONS

Skill Level: Beginner

Quilt Size: 62" x 72½"

Block Size: 4½" x 6"

Number of Blocks: 24

SUPPLIES

- Batting 68" x 79"
- All-purpose thread to match fabrics
- Quilting thread
- Basic sewing tools and supplies

COMPLETING THE BLOCKS

Step 1. Sew an E strip between two D strips with right sides together along the length to make a D-E-D strip set; press seams toward E. Repeat to make four strip sets.

Step 2. Subcut the D-E-D strip sets into (24) 6½" Lilac Stripe blocks referring to Figure 1.

6½"

Figure 1

COMPLETING THE QUILT

Step 1. Arrange and join the A, B and C rectangles

FABRIC Measurements based on 42" usable fabric width.	#STRIPS/ PIECES	CUT	#PIECES	SUBCUT
⅓ yard light green background lilac print	4	2" x 42" E		
⅞ yard blue background lilac print	3	6½" x 42"	24	5" C rectangles
	1	5" x 8" J rectangle		
⅞ yard cream background lilac print	3	6½" x 42"	24	5" B rectangles
	1	5" x 8" K rectangle		
⅞ yard dark green mottled	2	2½" x 42½" F		
	2	2½" x 36" G		
	7	2¼" x 42" binding		
1¾ yards lavender mottled	2	3" x 59" L along length		
	2	3" x 53½" M along length		
	2	2¼" x 46½" H along length		
	2	2¼" x 39½" I along length		
	8	2" x 42" D along length		
2 yards purple background lilac print	2	5" x 64" N along length		
	2	5" x 62½" O along length		
	1	6½" x 42" along length	8	5" A rectangles
Backing		68" x 79"		

with the Lilac Stripe blocks to make seven rows of seven units each referring to Figure 2; press seams away from the blocks.

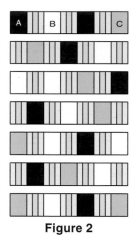

Figure 2

Step 2. Join the rows referring to the Placement Diagram for positioning; press seams in one direction.

Step 3. Sew F strips to opposite long sides and G strips to the top and bottom of the pieced center; press seams toward F and G strips. Repeat with H and I strips.

Step 4. Join three C and four B rectangles with the J rectangle to make a side border strip as shown in Figure 3; repeat with three B and four C rectangles and the K rectangle to make a second side border strip. Press seams in one direction.

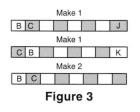

Figure 3

Step 5. Sew a side border strip to opposite long sides of the pieced center referring to the Placement Diagram for positioning of strips; press seams toward strips.

Step 6. Join four each B and C rectangles to make a top border strip, again referring to Figure 3; press seams in one direction. Repeat to make a bottom border strip.

Step 7. Sew the strips to the top and bottom of the pieced top referring to the Placement Diagram for positioning; press seams toward the H and I strips.

Step 8. Sew an L strip to opposite long sides and M strips to the top and bottom of the pieced center; press seams toward L and M strips. Repeat with N and O strips to complete the pieced top.

Step 9. Layer, quilt, prepare binding and bind edges referring to the Finishing Instructions. ■

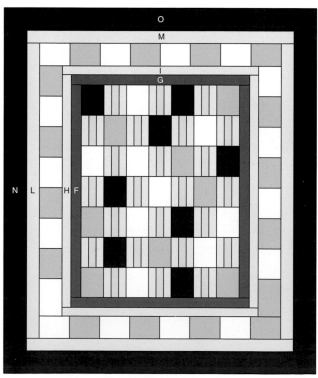

The Scent of Lilacs
Placement Diagram 62" x 72½"

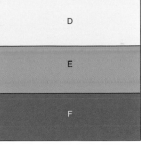

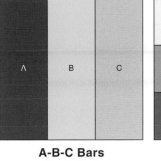

A-B-C Bars
6" x 6" Block
Make 32

D-E-F Bars
6" x 6" Block
Make 31

FANCY BARS

Design by Judith Sandstrom

Two color versions of one simple bar-design block take on a new look when sashed in this bed-size quilt.

PROJECT SPECIFICATIONS

Skill Level: Beginner
Quilt Size: 70" x 86"
Block Size: 6" x 6"
Number of Blocks: 63

SUPPLIES

- Batting 76" x 92"
- All-purpose thread to match fabrics
- Quilting thread
- Basic sewing tools and supplies

FABRIC Measurements based on 42" usable fabric width.	#STRIPS/PIECES	CUT	#PIECES	SUBCUT
¼ yard tan/blue print	4	6½" M squares		
⅓ yard dark green print	3	2½" x 42"	48	2½" H squares
½ yard each 6 contrasting fabrics	6	2½" x 42" each fabric for A–F		
⅔ yard tan tonal	8	2¼" x 42" binding		
1⅜ yards rose print	7	6½" x 42" K/L		
2 yards cream print	7	6½" x 42"	110	2½" G strips
	7	2½" x 42" I/J		
Backing		76" x 92"		

COMPLETING THE BLOCKS

Step 1. Label the contrasting fabric strips A–F.

Step 2. Sew an A strip to a B strip to a C strip with right sides together along the length; press seams in one direction. Repeat to complete six A-B-C strip sets.

Step 3. Subcut the A-B-C strip sets into (32) 6½" A-B-C Bars blocks as shown in Figure 1.

Step 4. Repeat Steps 2 and 3 with the D, E and F strips to complete 31 D-E-F Bars blocks, again referring to Figure 1.

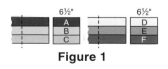

Figure 1

COMPLETING THE QUILT

Step 1. Join four A-B-C Bars blocks with three D-E-F Bars blocks and six G strips to make an X row as shown in Figure 2; press seams toward G strips. Repeat to make five X rows.

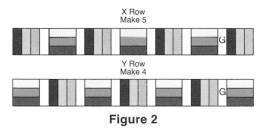

Figure 2

Step 2. Join four D-E-F Bars blocks with three A-B-C Bars blocks and six G strips to make a Y row, again referring to Figure 2; press seams toward G strips. Repeat to make four Y rows.

Step 3. Join seven G strips with six H squares to make a sashing row as shown in Figure 3; press seams toward G strips. Repeat to make eight sashing rows.

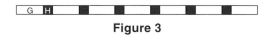

Figure 3

Step 4. Referring to the Placement Diagram, join the X and Y rows with the sashing rows to complete the pieced center; press seams toward the sashing rows.

Step 5. Join the I/J strips with right sides together on the short ends to make one long strip; press seams open. Subcut strip into two 70½" I strips and two 58½" J strips.

Step 6. Sew the I strips to opposite long sides and J strips to the top and bottom of the pieced center; press seams toward I and J strips.

Step 7. Join the K/L strips with right sides together on the short ends to make one long strip; press seams open. Subcut strips into two 74½" K strips and two 58½" L strips.

Step 8. Sew an M square to each end of the L strips; press seams toward L strips.

Step 9. Sew the K strips to opposite long sides and the L-M strips to the top and bottom of the pieced center; press seams toward K and L-M strips.

Step 10. Layer, quilt, prepare binding and bind edges referring to the Finishing Instructions to finish. ■

Fancy Bars
Placement Diagram 70" x 86"

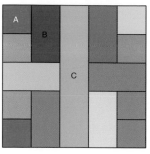

Almost Amish
10" x 10" Block
Make 12

ALMOST AMISH SCRAP QUILT

Design by Janet Jones Worley

This stunning wall quilt sparkles with jewel-tone Amish colors!

PROJECT SPECIFICATIONS

Skill Level: Beginner

Quilt Size: 40" x 50"

Block Size: 10" x 10"

Number of Blocks: 12

SUPPLIES

- Thin batting 46" x 56"
- Rotary-cutting tools
- All-purpose thread to blend with fabrics
- Black quilting thread
- Basic sewing tools and supplies

FABRIC Measurements based on 42" usable fabric width.	#STRIPS/PIECES	CUT
1⅝ yards total jewel-tone mottled scraps	96	2½" A squares
	72	2½" x 4½" B rectangles
	12	2½" x 10½" C rectangles
¾ yard dark red mottled	1	2½" x 40½" D
	1	2½" x 34½" F
	2	3½" x 42" I
	1	3½" x 40½" K
	6	2¼" x 21" binding
¾ yard black mottled	1	2½" x 40½" E
	1	2½" x 34½" G
	2	3½" x 42" H
	1	3½" x 40½" J
	6	2¼" x 21" binding
Backing		46" x 56"

COMPLETING THE BLOCKS

Step 1. Join two A squares in random colors to make 48 A units as shown in Figure 1; press seams to one side.

Figure 1

Step 2. Sew B to one side of each A unit as shown in Figure 2; press seams toward B. Repeat to make 48 A-B units.

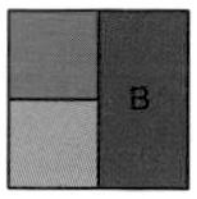

Figure 2

Step 3. Join two A-B units with B to make a block unit as shown in Figure 3; press seams toward B. Repeat to make 24 block units.

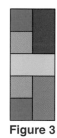

Figure 3

Step 4. Join two block units with C to complete one Almost Amish block referring to Figure 4; press seams toward C. Repeat to make 12 blocks.

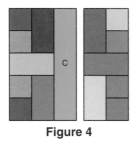

Figure 4

COMPLETING THE QUILT

Step 1. Arrange and join blocks in four rows of three blocks each, alternating the position of C referring to the Placement Diagram; press seams in adjacent rows in opposite directions.

Step 2. Referring to the Placement Diagram, sew the D strip to the right long side and E to the left long side of the pieced center; press seams toward D and E strips.

Step 3. Join H strips on short ends to make one long strip; press seams open. Subcut strip into one 44½" strip. Repeat with I strips.

Step 4. Repeat Step 2, adding the dark red and black border strips in alphabetical order referring to the Placement Diagram and press seams toward strips as added to complete the pieced top.

Step 5. Alternating lengths of dark red and black fabrics, prepare 5½ yards of binding; layer, quilt and bind edges referring to the Finishing Instructions. ■

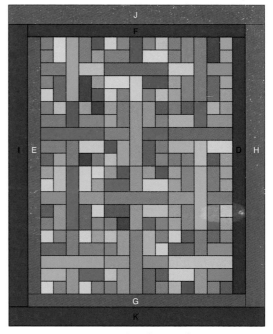

Almost Amish Scrap Quilt
Placement Diagram 40" x 50"

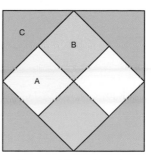

Framed Four-Patch
8½" x 8½" Block
Make 12

SCRAPPY FOUR-PATCH

Design by Johanna Wilson

Create a simple, effective springtime beauty with floral border strips.

PROJECT SPECIFICATIONS

Skill Level: Beginner

Quilt Size: 57" x 69"

Block Size: 8½" x 8½"

Number of Blocks: 12

SUPPLIES

- Batting 63" x 75"
- All-purpose thread to blend with fabrics
- Quilting thread
- Basic sewing tools and supplies

COMPLETING THE BLOCKS

Step 1. Sew A to B; press seam toward B. Repeat to make 24 A-B units.

Step 2. To complete one Framed Four-Patch block, join two A-B units to complete a center unit as shown in Figure 1; press seam in one direction.

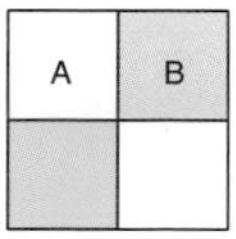

A	B

Figure 1

Step 3. Sew C to each side of the center unit to complete one block; press seams toward C. Repeat to make 12 Framed Four-Patch blocks.

FABRIC Measurements based on 42" usable fabric width.	#STRIPS/PIECES	CUT	#PIECES	SUBCUT
24 light scrap A squares 3½" x 3½"				
24 dark scrap B squares 3½" x 3½"				
1¼ yards total cream/tan scraps	5	13¼" squares		Cut each square on both diagonals to make 20 E triangles; discard 2
	6	6⅞" squares		Cut each square in half on 1 diagonal to make 12 D triangles
24 green scrap squares 5⅛" x 5⅛"				Cut each square in half on 1 diagonal to make 24 C triangles
⅓ yard rust print	6	1½" x 42" H		
½ yard green stripe	6	2½" x 42" I		
⅝ yard dark rust print	7	2¼" x 42" binding		
¾ yard floral	6	3½" x 42" J		
1½ yards coordinating floral border print	2	5" x 48½" F along the length of fabric		
	2	5" x 45½" G along the length of fabric		
Backing		63" x 75"		

COMPLETING THE QUILT

Step 1. Join Four Framed Four-Patch blocks with four D triangles and six E triangles to make a row as shown in Figure 2; press seams toward D and E. Repeat to make three rows.

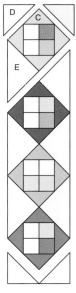

Figure 2

Step 2. Join the rows with the F strips and add G to the top and bottom to complete the pieced center; press seams toward F and G strips.

Step 3. Join the H strips on short ends to make one long strip; press seams open. Subcut strip into four 57½" H strips.

Step 4. Repeat Step 3 with I strips to subcut four 57½" I strips.

Step 5. Repeat Step 3 with J strips to subcut four 57½" J strips.

Step 6. Sew an H strip to an I strip to a J strip; press seams in one direction. Repeat to make four H-I-J strips.

Step 7. Sew an H-I-J strip to opposite long sides and then to the top and bottom of the pieced center to complete the pieced top; press seams toward the pieced strips.

Step 8. Layer, quilt, prepare binding and bind edges referring to the Finishing Instructions. ■

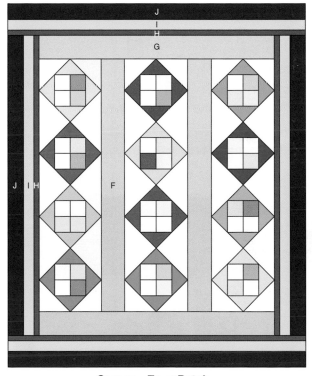

Scrappy Four-Patch
Placement Diagram 57" x 69"

RED, WHITE & BLUE AMERICANA

Design by Johanna Wilson

This table covering is picnic-perfect and easy to make!

PROJECT SPECIFICATIONS

Skill Level: Beginner

Tablecloth Size: 63" x 63"

SUPPLIES

- Thin batting 69" x 69"
- Rotary-cutting tools
- All-purpose thread to blend with fabrics
- Red, white and blue quilting thread
- Basic sewing tools and supplies

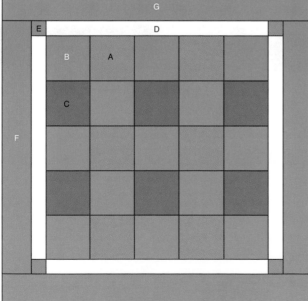

Red, White & Blue Americana
Placement Diagram 63" x 63"

FABRIC Measurements based on 42" usable fabric width.	#STRIPS/ PIECES	CUT	#PIECES	SUBCUT
¾ yard red print 1	2	9½" x 42"	6	9½" A squares
	4	3½" E squares		
1¼ yards red print 2	7	2¼ x 42" binding		
	2	9½" x 42"	6	9½" C squares
1½ yards accent stripe running along length	4	3½" x 45½" D strips along length of stripe		
3 yards red/white/ blue plaid	4	9½" x 42" along length of fabric	13	9½" B squares
	2	6½" x 51½" F along length of fabric		
	2	6½" x 63½" G along length of fabric		
Backing		69" x 69"		

COMPLETING THE TABLECLOTH

Step 1. Join two A squares with three B squares to make an X row as shown in Figure 1; press seams toward B squares. Repeat to make three X rows.

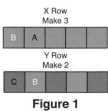

X Row
Make 3

Y Row
Make 2

Figure 1

Step 2. Join two B squares with three C squares to make a Y row, again referring to Figure 1; press seams toward B squares. Repeat to make two Y rows.

Step 3. Join the X and Y rows referring to the Placement Diagram to complete the pieced center; press seams in one direction.

Step 4. Sew D strips to opposite sides of the pieced center; press seams toward D strips.

Step 5. Sew an E square to each end of each remaining D strip; press seams toward D. Sew the D-E strips to the remaining sides of the pieced center; press seams toward the D-E strips.

Step 6. Sew an F strip to opposite sides and G strips to the remaining sides to complete the pieced center; press seams toward the F and G strips.

Step 7. Layer, quilt, prepare binding and bind edges referring to the Finishing Instructions. ■

NEVER THOUGHT YOU'D SEE A QUILT HERE

Most people think of quilts as bed coverings. Or they've been in the home of a quilter and discovered that quilts also decorate walls. It's time to expand your thinking! In this chapter, you'll find quilting on the fridge, quilting in the bathroom and quilting on a tissue cover. Where will you find it next?

FANCY NEEDLEWORK BASKET

Design by Mary Ayers

Use scraps of home-decorator fabrics and vintage
needlework to make an elegant needlework basket.

PROJECT SPECIFICATIONS

Skill Level: Beginner
Project Size: 7" x 4" x 5"

SUPPLIES

- All-purpose thread to match fabrics
- Quilting thread
- 1 yard ⅝"-wide ivory satin ribbon
- 5" x 8" rectangle heavy cardboard
- Basic sewing tools and supplies

FABRIC Measurements based on 42" usable fabric width.	#STRIPS/ PIECES	CUT
Scraps 5 floral print decorator fabrics	2	2½" x 5½" rectangle each fabric
¼ yard cream tonal decorator fabric for lining	2	5½" x 10½" rectangles
	2	Basket bottoms using pattern
8" ivory fabric doily with crocheted edging		

COMPLETING THE BASKET

Step 1. Select one 2½" x 5½" rectangle each floral
print fabric; join on the long edges to make a strip.
Press seams in one direction. Repeat to make two
identical strips.

Step 2. Join the strips on the 5½" ends to make a
tube; press seams to one side.

Step 3. Sew a basket bottom shape to the bottom
edge of the tube, aligning dots on pattern with side
seams of the tube.

Step 4. Center and baste the doily to the top front of
the assembled unit so it drapes in front, cutting off
excess doily that extends over the top edge.

Step 5. Cut ribbon into two 18" lengths. Fold ribbon
pieces in half and baste folded edges to top back of
basket, 2" in from each side.

Step 6. Sew the 5½" edges of the lining fabric
rectangles together.

Step 7. Sew the remaining basket bottom shape to
the bottom of the assembled lining rectangles, lining
up the dots on the pattern with side seams and leaving 4½" open in the center of one side.

Step 8. Turn the lining piece wrong side out; place
the basket shell right side out inside the lining,
matching side seams.

Step 9. Sew the basket shell to the lining along the top edge; turn the basket right side out through the opening in the lining.

Step 10. Cut cardboard shape along dotted lines on pattern; insert cardboard into basket through the opening in the lining. Place it so it fits snugly inside the basket bottom.

Step 11. Hand-stitch the lining opening closed.

Step 12. Wrap ribbon ties around a hanger (a large fork was used in sample project). Stitch through the center of the bows to secure. ■

Fancy Needlework Basket
Placement Diagram 7" x 4" x 5"

Basket Bottom
Cut 1 heavy cardboard without seam allowance & 2
cream tonal decorator fabric with seam allowance

QUILTED FRIDGE FRAMES

Designs by Nancy Richoux

Show off your grandchildren in a themed fridge frame.

PROJECT SPECIFICATIONS

Skill Level: Beginner

Frame Sizes: 14½" x 6½" and 14½" x 10½"

SUPPLIES

- All-purpose thread to match fabrics
- Quilting thread
- Brown and white embroidery floss
- 6 (¾") button magnets or adhesive magnetic strips for hanging
- Hot-glue gun with glue sticks
- 3½ yards ⅛"-wide tan satin ribbon
- Black and red fine-point fabric markers
- 3 (3½" x 5") photos
- 2 (2½" x 3½") photos
- Chalk pencil
- Tapestry needle
- Basic sewing tools and supplies

COMPLETING THE SPORTS FRAME

Step 1. Referring to Figure 1, draw three 3½" x 5" rectangles on A using a chalk pencil.

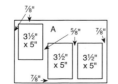

Figure 1

FABRIC Measurements based on 43" usable fabric width.	#STRIPS/ PIECES	CUT
Scraps brown, golden brown, green and white fabrics		Appliqué pieces as per patterns
Fat eighth multicolor print	2 2	¾" x 9" G ¾" x 17" H
Fat eighth light blue print	2 2	¾" x 13" B ¾" x 17" C
Fat quarter tan tonal	1 1	13½" x 9½" A 13½" x 5½" F
Fat quarter red mottled	1 2 2	18" x 10" backing 1" x 9" I 1" x 17" J Appliqué pieces as per patterns
Fat quarter royal blue print	1 2 2	18" x 14" backing 1" x 13" D 1" x 17" E
Flannel for batting		18" x 14" 18" x 10"

Step 2. Sew a B strip to a D strip; press seam toward D. Repeat to make two B-D strips. Repeat with C and E strips; press seams toward E.

Step 3. Center and sew a B-D strip to opposite short ends and C-E strips to opposite long edges of A, mitering corners as shown in Figure 2. Trim seam to ¼"; press seam open.

Figure 2

Step 4. Lightly trace the appliqué pieces of your choice from those given onto the right side of fabric scraps; cut out, leaving a ⅛"–¼" seam allowance beyond the marked lines.

Pick up
Amanda at
6 PM

Step 5. Turn under the edges of each appliqué shape and baste to hold.

Step 6. Add detail lines to each piece using red fabric marker for softball and black fabric marker for basketball and soccer ball; fill in several hexagons on the soccer ball with black fabric marker referring to the Placement Diagram. Using 2 strands white embroidery floss and a stem stitch, stitch detail lines on the football.

Step 7. Arrange and hand-stitch the appliqué pieces on A referring to the Placement Diagram and photo for placement. *Note: Do not place pieces inside or too close to the marked chalk lines.*

Step 8. Mark diagonal lines 1" apart across the top with chalk pencil as shown in Figure 3. *Note: Do not draw lines on appliqués or borders.*

Figure 3

Step 9. Sandwich the 18" x 14" flannel rectangle between the same-size backing piece and the appliquéd top; baste to hold layers together.

Step 10. Quilt on the marked lines and outline-quilt around the appliquéd shapes and in the ditch of border seams. Trim flannel even with edges of the quilted top. Trim backing ⅝" wider than quilted top.

Step 11. Press under ¼" on all sides of the backing piece. Bring the excess backing to the right side and hand-stitch in place on the outside border strips.

Step 12. Cut three 24" lengths of ⅛"-wide tan satin ribbon. Thread ribbon into a tapestry needle.

Step 13. Referring to Figure 4, pull ribbon through

from the back, 1" from the corner of a marked photo rectangle and ⅛" away from the marked line of number 1 and back down to the back at number 2, leaving a 4" tail on the back side. Repeat, coming up at 3 and down at 4, up at 5 and down at 6, and up at 7 and down at 8, always ⅛" away from the marked line. *Note: Be sure the ribbon lies flat and is not twisted. Tie ends in a square knot on the back side and trim. Repeat for all photo areas.*

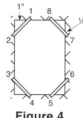

Figure 4

Step 14. Hot-glue three button magnets to the top of the project back.

Step 15. Tuck photos under ribbon corners and hang on a refrigerator or metal filing cabinet to display.

COMPLETING THE SCHOOLTIME FRIDGE FRAME

Step 1. Cut and prepare apple and leaf shapes for appliqué.

Step 2. Referring to Figure 5, mark the placement for two 2½" x 3½" photos on the F rectangle using a chalk pencil.

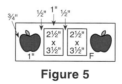

Figure 5

Step 3. Place an apple and leaf motif on each side of the marked lines, again referring to Figure 5 for positioning.

Step 4. Complete the appliqué as for the Sports

project; stem-stitch the stem lines using 3 strands brown embroidery floss.

Step 5. Sew a G strip to an I strip, and an H strip to a J strip; repeat to make two each G-I and H-J strips.

MITERING BORDER CORNERS

Making mitered corners on borders is a bit more difficult than adding butted border strips. Follow these simple steps to create a perfect miter every time.

Step 1. Join border strips; press seams toward darker fabric.

Step 2. Center and pin joined border strips on sides, and top and bottom of the center piece to which they will be stitched.

Step 3. Mark a dot ¼" from each side at each corner of center piece as shown in Photo 1.

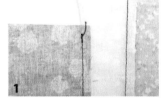

Step 4. Referring to Photo 2, sew center piece to borders starting at midpoint of sides, top and bottom and stopping at marked dot in corners of center piece.

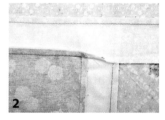

Step 5. Place on ironing surface right side up as shown in Photo 3.

Step 6. Complete the Schooltime Fridge Frame as for the Sports Fridge Frame using smaller flannel and backing pieces, two 24" lengths of ribbon and bringing ribbon up from back only ½" away from the corners of the marked photo rectangles. ■

Step 6. Take one border and fold it back at a 45-degree angle, making sure that the seams align as shown (Photo 4); press to make a crease in the border.

Step 7. Fold the project to make a 45-degree angle, pinning at seams to match; stitch on the creased lines on the strips as shown in Photos 5 and 6.

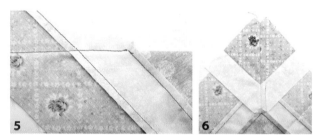

Step 8. Open to check stitching; if the strips align perfectly, trim excess strips to ¼" from stitching and press corner seam open to complete a perfect miter (Photo 7).

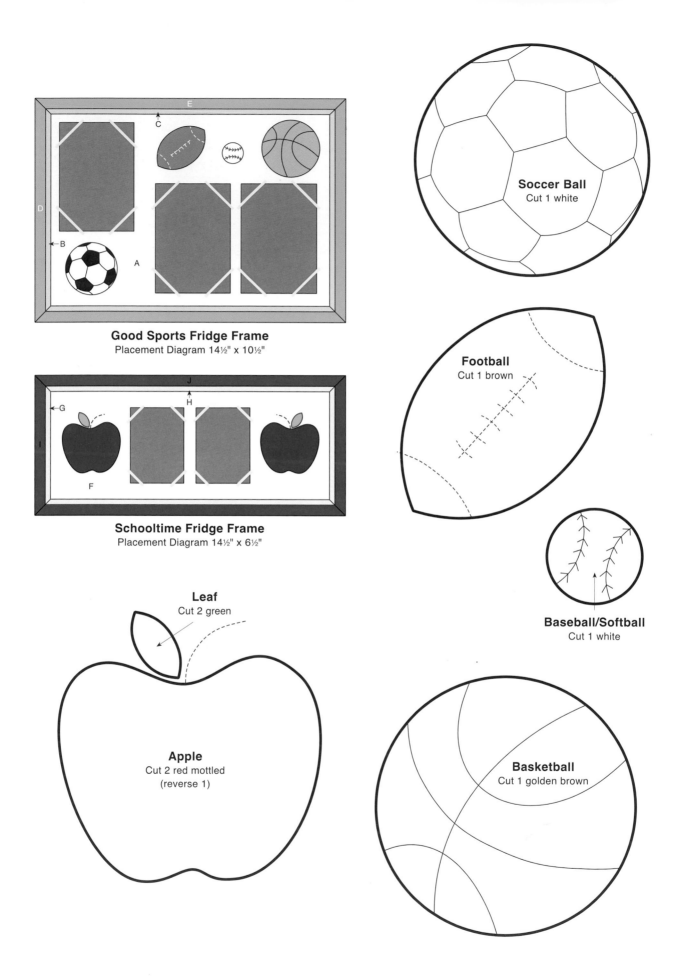

Good Sports Fridge Frame
Placement Diagram 14½" x 10½"

Schooltime Fridge Frame
Placement Diagram 14½" x 6½"

Soccer Ball
Cut 1 white

Football
Cut 1 brown

Baseball/Softball
Cut 1 white

Leaf
Cut 2 green

Apple
Cut 2 red mottled
(reverse 1)

Basketball
Cut 1 golden brown

Basketball
8" x 8" Block
Make 1

Soccer Ball
8" x 8" Block
Make 2

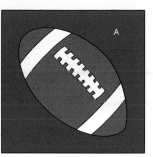

Football
8" x 8" Block
Make 2

ALL-SPORTS GROWTH CHART

Design by Barbara A. Clayton

Measure those little athletes to see how much they have grown from one sports season to the next.

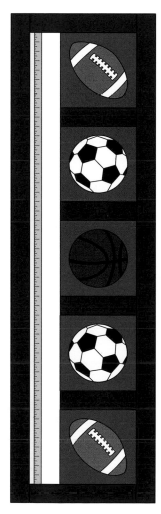

All-Sports Growth Chart
Placement Diagram 14½" x 52"

FABRIC Measurements based on 42" usable fabric width.	#STRIPS/ PIECES	CUT
⅛ yard black solid		Appliqué pieces as per patterns
¼ yard brown mottled		Appliqué pieces as per patterns
¼ yard brown speckled		Appliqué pieces as per patterns
¼ yard white solid		Appliqué pieces as per patterns
⅝ yard blue plaid	5	8½" A squares
⅝ yard red-with-white dots	4	2½" x 8½" B
	2	2½" x 11" C
	3	2½" x 42" F
1½ yards cream print	1	1¼" x 48½" E along length
	4	2¼" x 42" binding
1¾ yards muslin	1	3" x 48½" D along length
	1	21" x 58" backing
	1	2½" x 15" sleeve

PROJECT SPECIFICATIONS

Skill Level: Intermediate

Chart Size: 14½" x 52"

Block Size: 8" x 8"

Number of Blocks: 5

SUPPLIES

- Batting 21" x 58"
- All-purpose thread to match fabrics
- Quilting thread
- Clear nylon monofilament
- ½ yard fusible web
- ¾ yard fabric stabilizer
- ¾"-wide at least 64"-long yellow measuring tape
- Basting spray
- Basic sewing tools and supplies

COMPLETING THE BLOCKS

Step 1. Trace appliqué motifs onto the paper side of the fusible web referring to the patterns for number to cut. Cut out shapes, leaving a margin around each one.

Step 2. Fuse paper shapes to the wrong side of fabrics as directed on patterns for color and number to cut; cut out shapes on traced lines. Remove paper patterns.

Step 3. Center and fuse a basketball motif to A, being careful to layer the black trim pieces in numerical order as marked on pattern.

Step 4. Repeat Step 3 to fuse two each soccer ball and football motifs.

Step 5. Cut five 8" x 8" squares stabilizer; spray-baste a square to the wrong side of each fused block.

Step 6. Using thread to match fabrics, stitch on all detail lines and around edges of each shape with a close machine satin stitch. When stitching is complete, remove fabric stabilizer to complete one Basketball and two each Football and Soccer Ball blocks.

Trim
Cut 2
white solid
(reverse 1)

Laces
Cut 2 white solid

Football Motif
Cut 2 brown mottled

COMPLETING THE CHART

Step 1. Arrange and join the balls in a vertical row with B strips referring to the Placement Diagram; press seams toward B strips.

Step 2. Place the E strip right side up on the D strip with left long edge aligned as shown in Figure 1; baste the inner raw edges of the E strip in place on D, again referring to Figure 1.

Step 3. Lay the measuring tape over the D-E strip ¾" from the left side edge and 1½" from the right side edge as shown in Figure 2, concealing the inner raw edge of the E strip and starting the measuring tape at the 15¾" mark at the bottom of the strip and stopping at the 64¼" mark at the top, again referring to Figure 2.

Figure 2

Align on this edge.

E | D

Figure 1

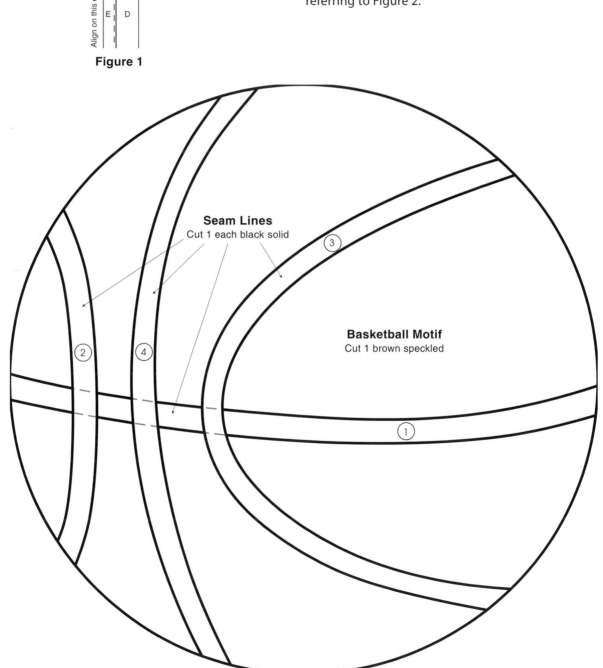

Seam Lines
Cut 1 each black solid

③

② ④

Basketball Motif
Cut 1 brown speckled

①

Step 4. Machine blind-hem-stitch the measuring tape in place using clear nylon monofilament in the top of the machine and all-purpose thread to match E in the bobbin.

Step 5. Trim excess measuring tape at the top and bottom. *Note: Use the D strip to write the date of your child's height after each measurement.*

Step 6. Sew the D-E-tape strip to the left side edge of the pieced center; press seam away from the pieced center.

Step 7. Join the F strips with right sides together on

short ends to make one long strip; press seams open. Subcut strip into two 52½" F strips.

Step 8. Sew a C strip to the top and bottom, and F strips to opposite long sides of the pieced center to complete the pieced top; press seams toward C and F strips.

Step 9. Layer, quilt, prepare binding and bind edges referring to the Finishing Instructions.

Step 10. Refer to page 175 for instructions on making and applying a hanging sleeve to finish. ■

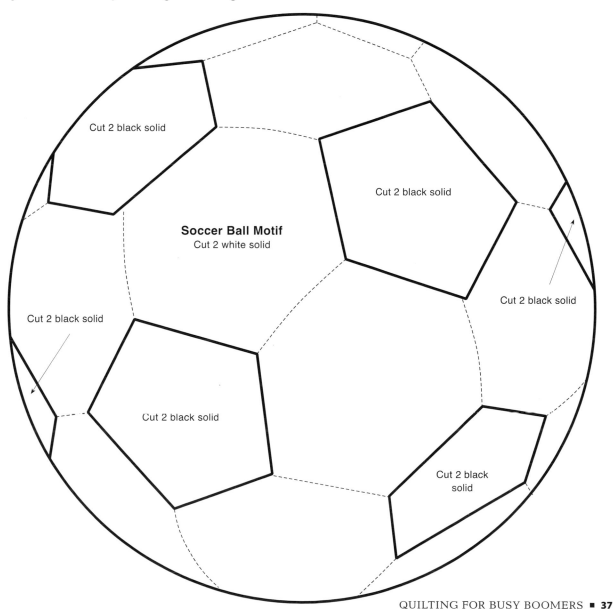

Cut 2 black solid

Cut 2 black solid

Soccer Ball Motif
Cut 2 white solid

Cut 2 black solid

Cut 2 black solid

Cut 2 black solid

Cut 2 black solid

Trailing Ivy Roll Holder
Placement Diagram
5¼" x 5¼"

TRAILING IVY ROLL HOLDER

Design by Barbara A. Clayton

Keep an extra roll of toilet paper hidden away under this coordinating holder.

PROJECT SPECIFICATIONS

Skill Level: Intermediate

Holder Size: 5¼" x 5¼"

SUPPLIES

- Batting 7" x 20"
- All-purpose thread to match fabrics
- 1 spool clear nylon monofilament
- Dark green and white quilting thread
- ⅛ yard medium-weight fusible interfacing
- ⅛ yard tear-off fabric stabilizer
- 18" (⅛"-wide) dark green ribbon
- 42-ounce oatmeal box
- Hot-glue gun and glue sticks
- Water-erasable marker or pen
- Knitting needle or stylet (this is for turning leaves-see next pattern)
- Safety pins
- Basic sewing tools and supplies

INSTRUCTIONS

Step 1. Sew B to each 17" side of A; press seams toward B.

Step 2. Sew a C strip to each long side of the pieced section. Press seams toward C strips.

Step 3. Prepare ivy leaves referring to Preparing

FABRIC Measurements based on 42" usable fabric width.	#STRIPS/ PIECES	CUT
⅛ yard medium green print	1	1½" x 17" B
⅛ yard off-white solid	1	2¾" x 17" A
⅓ yard dark green solid	2	1" x 17" C
	1	5½" x 17" D
	1	1¼" x 4½" loop Appliqué pieces as per patterns, Circle piece E as per pattern
Backing		7" x 20"

Appliqué Pieces for Trailing Ivy Tissue Box Cover on page 41 and using small and large leaf patterns on page 43; cut number as directed on patterns.

Step 4. Arrange prepared leaf motifs on A, overlapping onto the B strips on both sides referring to Figure 1. Appliqué in place and embroider stems using a wide, close zigzag stitch referring to the Placement Diagram for positioning.

Figure 1

Step 5. Layer the stitched top with the batting and backing pieces and quilt as desired by hand or machine. Trim excess backing and batting even with pieced and appliquéd section.

Step 6. Using quilted section as a pattern, cut a lining piece from dark green solid.

Step 7. Sew the lining to one long side of the quilted piece; press seam toward lining.

Step 8. Join the quilted strip/lining right sides together on short ends to make a tube as shown in Figure 2; press seam open. Turn right side out.

Figure 2

Step 9. Join the stem lines at the seam area using same method as when stitching stems.

Step 10. Prepare template for E using pattern piece given; cut as directed on the pattern. Pin the circle to the dark

green solid end of the tube with right sides together; stitch around with a ¼" seam. Turn right side out.

Step 11. Cut the oatmeal box 5¼" up from the bottom all the way around. Cut a circle dark green solid using box bottom as pattern; hot-glue to the outside of the box bottom.

Step 12. Put some hot glue on the inside of the box bottom; pull the quilted roll cover over the open end of the box, pushing the lining inside the box and gluing the E circle to the inside box bottom. Turn box bottom side up. ***Note:*** *The ends of the quilted section should extend slightly above the edge of the box.*

Step 13. Fold the D strip in half along length with right sides together. Stitch short ends together to make a tube, leaving ½" open at folded edge to insert the 18" dark green ribbon for gathering as shown in Figure 3. Press seam open; turn right side out.

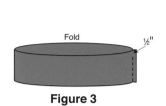

Figure 3

Figure 4

Step 14. Pull tube down over box, aligning raw edges with raw edges of quilted top and aligning side seams as shown in Figure 4. Stitch around just above box edge; bring tube section up over top of box.

Step 15. Insert the dark green ribbon through the opening in the top by the folded edge by pinning a safety pin to the end and pushing it through.

Step 16. Pull both ends of the ribbon tightly to gather the roll holder top together. Tie in a knot and push inside to hide.

Step 17. Turn under each long edge of loop strip ¼"; press. Fold strip in half along length with wrong sides together and pressed edges inside. Stitch along edge as shown in Figure 5.

Figure 5

Step 18. Push ends inside gathered opening; hand-stitch ends in place letting loop extend outside opening to finish. ■

E
Cut 1 dark green solid

TRAILING IVY TISSUE BOX COVER

Design by Barbara A. Clayton

Hide your tissue box under this quilted cover and place it where everyone can find it in a hurry.

PROJECT SPECIFICATIONS

Tissue Box Cover Size: Approximately 5" x 5" x 5½"

SUPPLIES

- 5½" x 5½" square and 8" x 22" rectangle batting
- All-purpose thread to match fabrics
- 1 spool clear nylon monofilament
- Dark green and white quilting thread
- ¼ yard medium-weight fusible interfacing
- ⅓ yard tear-off fabric stabilizer
- Lightweight poster board
- Hot-glue gun and glue sticks
- Knitting needle or stylet
- Water-erasable marker or pen
- Basic sewing tools and supplies

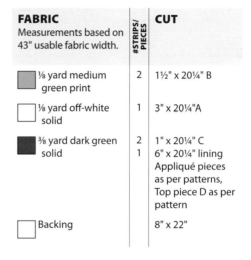

FABRIC Measurements based on 43" usable fabric width.	#STRIPS/PIECES	CUT
⅛ yard medium green print	2	1½" x 20¼" B
⅛ yard off-white solid	1	3" x 20¼" A
⅜ yard dark green solid	2 1	1" x 20¼" C 6" x 20¼" lining Appliqué pieces as per patterns, Top piece D as per pattern
Backing		8" x 22"

PREPARING APPLIQUÉ PIECES

Step 1. Prepare templates for small and large leaf patterns found on page 43. Transfer cutting instructions to templates.

Step 2. Cut shapes as indicated on pattern piece for number and color, adding a ¼" seam allowance to each piece. Cut an identical shape from lightweight fusible interfacing for each fabric piece needed.

Step 3. Pin the appliqué pieces right sides together with the fusible side of the lightweight fusible interfacing pieces; stitch all around seam allowance. Clip curves; trim seams to ¼".

Step 4. Make a small slit in the center of the interfacing side only; turn right side out through the slit. Smooth seams using a knitting needle or stylet. ***Note:*** *The fusible side of the interfacing should be on the outside.*

COMPLETING THE COVER

Step 1. Sew the A strip between the two B strips as shown in Figure 1; press seams away from A. Add C, again referring to Figure 1.

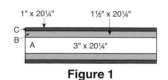

Figure 1

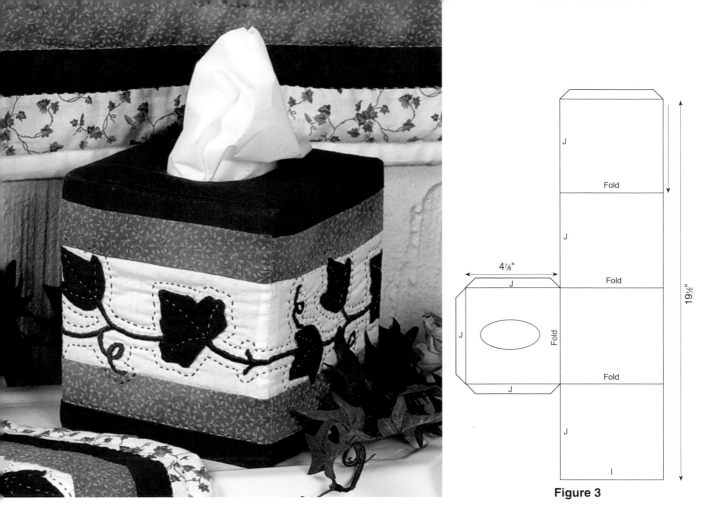

J

Fold

J

4⅞"

J

Fold

Fold

J

Fold

J

Fold

J

I

19½"

Figure 3

Step 2. Arrange prepared leaf motifs on A, overlapping onto the B strips on both sides referring to Figure 2. Appliqué in place and embroider stems using a wide, close zigzag stitch referring to Placement Diagram for positioning.

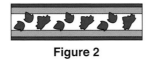

Figure 2

Step 3. Layer the stitched top with the batting and backing pieces and quilt as desired by hand or machine. Trim excess backing and batting even with pieced and appliquéd section.

Step 4. Join the quilted strip right sides together on short ends to make a tube; press seam open.

Step 5. Join the stem lines at the seam area using same method as when stitching stems.

Step 6. Prepare template for D; cut as directed on

piece. Pin the two fabric squares right sides together; place batting square under one piece. Stitch around oval opening on marked seam line. Trim away center fabric close to stitching line.

Step 7. Clip curves; turn right side out. Press center opening seam lightly.

Step 8. Divide the raw-edge top of quilted tube into four equal parts, clipping each mark to slightly under ¼". Pin the top fabric and batting (not lining) right sides together with the quilted tube, pinning the four corners to the four clipped marks; sew seam.

Step 9. Sew the ends of the lining strip together to make a tube. Divide into four equal parts as for quilted tube and pin; stitch to the lining side of the top piece.

Step 10. Referring to Figure 3, cut tissue box cover shape from the lightweight poster board. Lightly score fold lines using straightedge and stylet or knitting needle. Fold each fold line; cut out the center oval from the top of the box.

Step 11. Using hot-glue gun, glue the H tab to I, and the top J tabs to the inside of the J sides of the box.

Step 12. Pull the quilted tissue box cover over the top of the poster board box, pushing the lining through the center oval opening. Hot-glue the lining to the top inside of the box. Fold the raw edges of the lining over the bottom edge of the box and hand-stitch the quilted cover to the folded edges of the lining all the way around to finish. ■

Trailing Ivy Tissue Box Cover
Placement Diagram Approximately 5" x 5" x 5½"

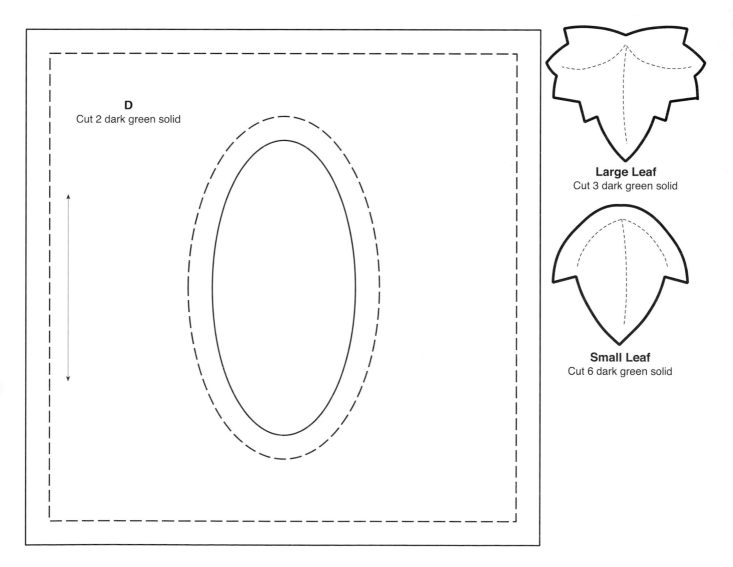

D
Cut 2 dark green solid

Large Leaf
Cut 3 dark green solid

Small Leaf
Cut 6 dark green solid

APPLIQUÉ QUILTS ADD A WHOLE NEW DIMENSION

If you have only pieced quilt tops, it's time to add appliqué to your repertoire. If you are still a busy mom and grandmother, try fusible appliqué—an iron, some fusible web and you're in business. There are those who swear by the therapeutic effects of hand appliqué. Either way, enjoy!

MACHINE SATIN-STITCH USING STABILIZER

Stabilizers are used in appliqué to prevent the base fabric from distorting during the machine-appliqué process. Other uses include holding fabric fibers in place, supporting stitches and maintaining the integrity of dense areas of embellishment of all kinds.

Stabilizers are available by the yard, roll, packages or in sheets. They can be fusible, adhesive or held in place with a temporary spray adhesive or pins (Photo 1).

Tear-away stabilizer is most commonly used with woven, stable fabrics. It is torn away when stitching is complete.

Melt-away/heat-away stabilizers are removed with the heat of an iron that turns them into ash that is brushed away. Water-soluble stabilizers disappear when soaked or washed.

Photo 2 illustrates an area on the left stitched with fabric stabilizer and one on the right stitched without. Notice the puckering that occurs on the area without the stabilizer.

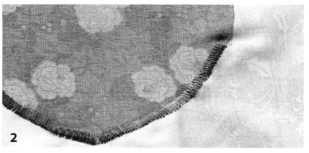

USING FABRIC STABILIZER

Step 1. Apply appliqué shapes or motifs to the background referring to the specific project instructions and drawings for positioning.

Step 2. Apply stabilizer to the wrong side of the background block referring to the manufacturer's instructions.

Step 3. Select matching or contrasting thread of choice and thread your machine and bobbin. *Note: There is a special thread available for use in the bobbin for machine appliqué.*

Step 4. Set your sewing machine to sew a satin stitch; adjust width and density desired.

Step 5. Stitch around each motif, starting with piece No. 1 if pattern motif is numbered, changing thread, as desired.

Step 6. When all stitching is complete, remove fabric stabilizer referring to manufacturer's instructions. *Note: The sample shown in Photo 3 uses a tear-off stabilizer.*

USING AN APPLIQUÉ PRESSING SHEET

The Appliqué Pressing Sheet is a 13" x 17" flexible sheet of high-temperature woven glass coated with nonstick Polylon. It is double-sided, heat-tolerant and transparent. It is used to accurately layer fused appliqué shapes to create a complete motif before placing on fabric.

Step 1. Lay the reverse appliqué pattern diagram flat on an ironing board. ***Note:*** *Many appliqué patterns are given in reverse for fusible appliqué; if they are not, simply trace the pattern given, turn the paper over and trace the pattern from the other side to make a reverse pattern.*

Step 2. Place the pressing sheet over the motif and anchor the corners of both with straight pins (Photo 1).

Step 3. Remove the paper backing from the appliqué pieces and assemble the design by matching the pieces to the diagram in numerical order, fusing sections of pieces as you go to complete the motif (Photos 2, 3 and 4).

Step 4. When finished, allow the appliqué motif to cool for a few seconds; peel it off the pressing sheet. The design is now in one piece, which makes it so much easier to fuse to the background fabric (Photo 5).

Nine-Patch
6" x 6" Block
Make 5

Posie
6" x 6" Block
Make 4

POSIE PARTY

Design by Jill Reber

Nine-Patch and Posie blocks combine in this
quick-to-stitch topper.

PROJECT SPECIFICATIONS

Skill Level: Beginner

Quilt Size: 22" x 22"

Block Size: 6" x 6"

Number of Blocks: 9

SUPPLIES

- Batting 28" x 28"
- All-purpose thread to match fabrics
- Quilting thread
- ½ yard fusible web
- Basic sewing tools and supplies

APPLIQUÉ CUTTING

Step 1. Trace appliqué shapes given onto the paper
side of the fusible web; cut out shapes, leaving a
margin around each one.

Step 2. Fuse the flower shapes to the wrong side
of the hot pink squares and the leaf shapes to the
wrong side of the green dot scrap. Cut out shapes
on traced lines; remove paper backing.

COMPLETING THE NINE-PATCH BLOCKS

Step 1. Sew an A strip to a B strip to
an A strip with right sides together
along the length; press seams toward
the A strips. Subcut strip set into (10)
2½" A-B units as shown in Figure 1.

Figure 1

FABRIC Measurements based on 42" usable fabric width.	#STRIPS/ PIECES	CUT	#PIECES	SUBCUT
4" x 10" scrap green dot		Appliqué pieces as per patterns		
4 (5") squares hot pink scraps		Appliqué pieces as per patterns		
⅓ yard pink print	2	2½" x 42" A		
	1	2½" x 21" half-A		
	1	2½" x 21"	4	2½" E squares
⅓ yard pink plaid	3	2¼" x 42" binding		
⅝ yard white tonal	1	2½" x 42" B		
	2	2½" x 21" half-B		
	1	6½" x 42"	4	6½" C squares
	2	2½" x 42"	4	18½" D strips
Backing		28" x 28"		

Step 2. Sew a half-B strip to a half-A strip to a half-B strip
with right sides together along the length; press seams
toward the half-A strip. Subcut the strip set into five 2½"
B-A units, again referring to Figure 1.

Step 3. Sew a B-A unit between two A-B units to
complete one Nine-Patch block referring to the block
drawing; press seams in one direction. Repeat to
make five Nine-Patch blocks.

COMPLETING THE POSIE BLOCKS

Step 1. To complete one Posie block, arrange and fuse
a flower and leaf shape on a C square, tucking the end
of the leaf under the flower, as indicated on pattern,
before fusing. Repeat to complete four Posie blocks.

COMPLETING THE QUILT

Step 1. Sew a Posie block between two Nine-Patch blocks to make an X row; press seams toward the Posie block. Repeat to make two X rows.

Step 2. Sew a Nine-Patch block between two Posie blocks to make a Y row; press seams toward Posie blocks.

Step 3. Sew the Y row between the two X rows to complete the pieced center; press seams toward the Y row.

Step 4. Sew an E square to each end of two D strips; press seams away from E.

Step 5. Sew a D strip to opposite sides and a D-E strip to the remaining sides of the pieced center to complete the top; press seams toward D and D-E strips.

Step 6. Layer, quilt, prepare binding and bind edges referring to the Finishing Instructions.

Step 7. Using a medium-width machine zigzag stitch and thread to match fabrics, stitch around the edges of the flower and leaf shapes to finish. ■

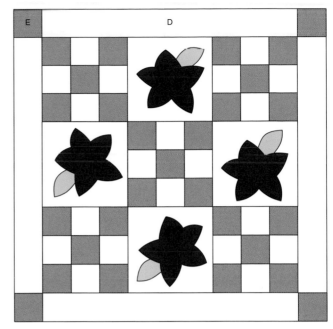

Posie Parade
Placement Diagram 22" x 22"

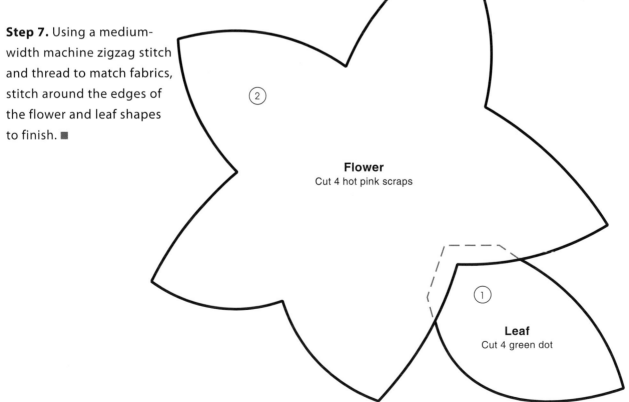

Flower
Cut 4 hot pink scraps

Leaf
Cut 4 green dot

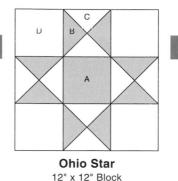

Ohio Star
12" x 12" Block
Make 20

PRETTY IN PINK

Design by Doris Nowell

Hexagon flowers cover the intersections of the Ohio Star blocks. This makes it hard to tell where one block ends and another begins.

PROJECT SPECIFICATIONS

Skill Level: Intermediate

Quilt Size: 48" x 60"

Block Size: 12" x 12"

Number of Blocks: 20

SUPPLIES

- Batting 54" x 66"
- All-purpose thread to match fabrics
- Quilting thread
- Card stock
- Basic sewing tools and supplies

COMPLETING THE OHIO STAR BLOCKS

Step 1. Select one A square and eight B triangles to match A.

FABRIC Measurements based on 42" usable fabric width.	#STRIPS/ PIECES	CUT	#PIECES	SUBCUT
⅛ yard each 12 different pink fabrics	6	E hexagons each fabric		
¼ yard each 20 different pink fabrics	1	4½" A square each fabric		
	2	5¼" squares each fabric		Cut each square on both diagonals to make 8 B triangles each fabric
2½ yards white solid	9	4½" x 42"	80	4½" D squares
	5	5¼" x 42"	40	5¼" squares; cut each square on both diagonals to make 160 C triangles
	12	E hexagons		
	6	2¼" x 42" binding		
Backing		54" x 66"		

Step 2. To complete one Ohio Star block, sew B to C as shown in Figure 1; press seam toward B. Repeat to make eight B-C units.

Figure 1

Figure 2

Step 3. Join two B-C units to complete a side unit as shown in Figure 2; press seam in one direction. Repeat to make four side units.

Step 4. Sew a side unit to opposite sides of A to make the center row as shown in Figure 3; press seams toward A.

Figure 3   **Figure 4**

Step 5. Sew D to opposite sides of a side unit to make a row as shown in Figure 4; press seams toward D. Repeat to make two rows; sew the rows to opposite sides of the center row to complete one block. Press seams toward the center row.

Step 6. Repeat Steps 1–5 to complete 19 more Ohio Star blocks.

COMPLETING THE HEXAGON FLOWERS

Step 1. Center a card-stock E on each fabric E; carefully fold the fabric seam allowance over one edge of the card-stock piece as shown in Figure 5. Finger-press to hold; repeat on all sides.

Figure 5

Step 2. Baste close to the folded edge as shown in Figure 6. Repeat for all E pieces.

Figure 6

Step 3. To complete one hexagon flower, select one white solid E and six matching pink E's.

Step 4. Whipstitch the six pink E hexagons together along the edges, inserting the white solid E in the center as shown in Figure 7. Repeat to make 12 hexagon flowers.

Figure 7

Step 5. Remove basting and card-stock pieces.

COMPLETING THE QUILT

Step 1. Join four Ohio Star blocks to make a row; press seams in one direction. Repeat to make five rows.

Step 2. Join the rows, alternating the direction of the pressed seams in adjacent rows; press seams in one direction.

Pretty in Pink
Placement Diagram 48" x 60"

Step 3. Center a hexagon flower on the D squares at the intersection of the blocks as shown in Figure 8; hand-stitch in place.

Figure 8

Step 4. Layer, quilt, prepare binding and bind edges referring to the Finishing Instructions to finish. ∎

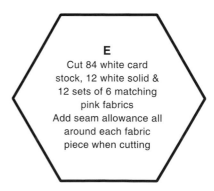

E
Cut 84 white card
stock, 12 white solid &
12 sets of 6 matching
pink fabrics
Add seam allowance all
around each fabric
piece when cutting

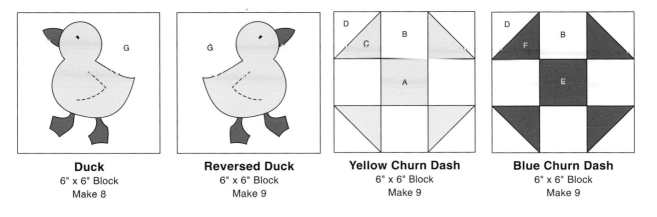

Duck
6" x 6" Block
Make 8

Reversed Duck
6" x 6" Block
Make 9

Yellow Churn Dash
6" x 6" Block
Make 9

Blue Churn Dash
6" x 6" Block
Make 9

DUCKS IN A ROW

Design by Jill Reber

Appliqué and piecing combine in this yellow-and-blue baby quilt.

PROJECT SPECIFICATIONS

Skill Level: Beginner

Quilt Size: 44" x 56"

Block Size: 6" x 6"

Number of Blocks: 35

SUPPLIES

- Batting 50" x 62"
- All-purpose thread to match fabrics
- Quilting thread
- ¾ yard fusible web
- 1⅛ yards fabric stabilizer, cut into 18 (6" x 6") squares
- Basic sewing tools and supplies

APPLIQUÉ

Step 1. Trace appliqué shapes on page 153 onto the paper side of the fusible web; cut out shapes, leaving a margin around each one.

Step 2. Fuse the shapes to the wrong side of the fabrics as directed on each piece for color. Cut out shapes on traced lines; remove paper backing.

Step 3. Center one duck motif on G, placing pieces in numerical order; fuse in place. Repeat to fuse eight duck and nine reversed duck motifs.

FABRIC Measurements based on 42" usable fabric width.	#STRIPS/ PIECES	CUT	#PIECES	SUBCUT
⅛ yard orange tonal		Appliqué pieces as per patterns		
¼ yard yellow print	1	2½" x 42"	9	2½" A squares
	2	2⅞" x 42"	18	2⅞" squares; cut in half on 1 diagonal to make 36 C triangles
⅓ yard yellow tonal		Appliqué pieces as per patterns		
¾ yard blue dot	1	2½" x 42"	9	2½" E squares
	2	2⅞" x 42"	18	2⅞" squares; cut in half on 1 diagonal to make 36 F triangles
	6	2¼" x 42" binding		
1 yard blue-and-yellow print	2	5½" x 34½" J		
	3	5½" x 42" K		
2½ yards white tonal	5	2½" x 42"	72	2½" B squares
	3	2⅞" x 42"	36	2⅞" squares; cut in half on 1 diagonal to make 72 D triangles
	5	6½" x 42"	17	6½" G squares
	2	2½" x 30½" H		
	3	2½" X 42" I		
Backing		50" x 62"		

Step 4. Pin a square of stabilizer to the wrong side of each duck-motif square.

Step 5. Machine satin-stitch around each appliqué shape and stitch detail lines using matching thread. Satin-stitch an eye using orange thread; remove fabric stabilizer when stitching is complete.

COMPLETING THE CHURN DASH BLOCKS

Step 1. Sew C to D to complete a C-D unit as shown in Figure 1; repeat to make 36 C-D units. Press seams toward C.

Figure 1

Step 2. Repeat with F and D to complete 36 D-F units, again referring to Figure 1; press seams toward F.

Step 3. To complete one Yellow Churn Dash block, sew B to opposite sides of A; press seams toward A.

Step 4. Sew a C-D unit to opposite sides of B; press seams toward C-D. Repeat to make two B-C-D rows.

Step 5. Sew a B-C-D row to opposite sides of the A-B row to complete one block referring to the Yellow Churn Dash block drawing. Repeat to make nine blocks.

Step 6. Repeat Steps 3–5 with B, D–F and E pieces referring to Figure 2 to complete nine Blue Churn Dash blocks.

Figure 2

COMPLETING THE QUILT

Step 1. Arrange and join the blocks in rows referring to Figure 3; press seams away from the appliquéd blocks.

Make 2
Make 1
Make 1
Make 1
Make 2

Figure 3

Step 2. Arrange and join the rows referring to the Placement Diagram to complete the pieced center.

Step 3. Sew an H strip to the top and bottom of the pieced center; press seams toward H strips.

Step 4. Join I strips on short ends to make one long strip; press seams open. Subcut strip into two 46½" I strips.

Step 5. Sew an I strip to opposite long sides of the pieced center; press seams toward I strips.

Step 6. Sew a J strip to the top and bottom of the pieced center; press seams toward J strips.

Step 7. Join K strips on short ends to make one long strip; press seams open. Subcut strip into two 56½" K strips.

Step 8. Sew K strips to opposite long sides of the pieced center; press seams toward K strips.

Step 9. Layer, quilt, prepare binding and bind edges referring to the Finishing Instructions to finish. ■

Ducks in a Row
Placement Diagram
44" x 56"

ROOSTER WALL QUILT

Design by Barbara A. Clayton

A checkerboard border surrounds the appliquéd rooster on this kitchen wall quilt.

PROJECT SPECIFICATIONS

Skill Level: Beginner

Quilt Size: 18½" x 23½"

SUPPLIES

- Batting 24" x 29"
- All-purpose thread to match fabrics
- Clear nylon monofilament for quilting
- Black embroidery floss
- ½ yard fusible web
- 9" x 9" square fabric stabilizer
- Basic sewing tools and supplies

APPLIQUÉ

Step 1. Trace appliqué shapes given onto the paper side of the fusible web; cut out shapes, leaving a margin around each one.

Step 2. Fuse the shapes to the wrong side of the scraps as directed on each piece for color. Cut out shapes on traced lines; remove paper backing.

Step 3. Arrange appliqué shapes on A in numerical order, overlapping as necessary. When satisfied with placement, fuse shapes in place.

Step 4. Pin fabric stabilizer square to the wrong side of the fused A.

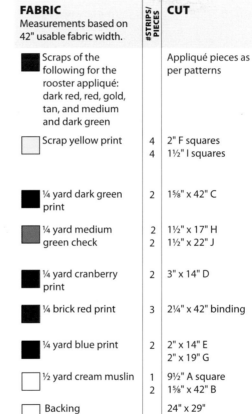

FABRIC Measurements based on 42" usable fabric width.	#STRIPS/ PIECES	CUT
Scraps of the following for the rooster appliqué: dark red, red, gold, tan, and medium and dark green		Appliqué pieces as per patterns
Scrap yellow print	4 4	2" F squares 1½" I squares
¼ yard dark green print	2	1⅝" x 42" C
¼ yard medium green check	2 2	1½" x 17" H 1½" x 22" J
¼ yard cranberry print	2	3" x 14" D
¼ brick red print	3	2¼" x 42" binding
¼ yard blue print	2	2" x 14" E 2" x 19" G
½ yard cream muslin	1 2	9½" A square 1⅝" x 42" B
Backing		24" x 29"

Step 5. Using thread to match fabrics and a machine blanket stitch, stitch around the edge of each fused piece to hold in place; remove fabric stabilizer.

Step 6. Using 2 strands black embroidery floss, satin-stitch the eye as marked on the pattern.

COMPLETING THE TOP

Step 1. Sew a B strip to a C strip with right sides together along the length; press seams toward the C strip. Repeat to make two B-C strip sets. Subcut strip sets into (40) 1⅝" B-C units as shown in Figure 1.

Figure 1

Step 2. Join eight B-C units to make a side strip as shown in Figure 2; repeat to make two side strips. Press seams in one direction.

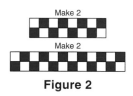

Figure 2

Step 3. Sew a side strip to opposite sides of the appliqué A square; press seams toward side strips.

Step 4. Repeat Step 2 to join 12 B-C units to make the top strip, again referring to Figure 2; repeat to make the bottom strip. Press seams in one direction. Sew a strip to the top and bottom of A; press seams toward the strips.

Step 5. Sew a D strip to the top and bottom, and G strips to opposite long sides of the pieced center; press seams toward D and G strips.

Step 6. Sew an F square to each end of each E strip; press seams toward E. Sew these strips to the D sides of the pieced center; press seams toward the D-E strips.

Step 7. Repeat Steps 5 and 6 with J strips on opposite long sides and H-I strips on the top and bottom of the pieced center; press seams toward J and H-I strips to complete the pieced top.

Step 8. Layer, quilt, prepare binding and bind edges referring to the Finishing Instructions.

Step 9. Hand- or machine-quilt as desired to finish. *Note: The quilt shown was machine-quilted using clear nylon monofilament around the appliqué motifs and in the ditch between border seams and using thread to match fabrics in a crosshatch design in D. A fabric sleeve or plastic rings may be added to the top back for hanging.* ■

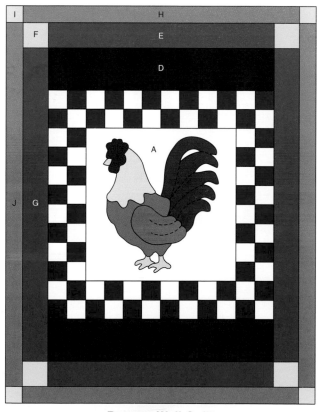

Rooster Wall Quilt
Placement Diagram 18½" x 23½"

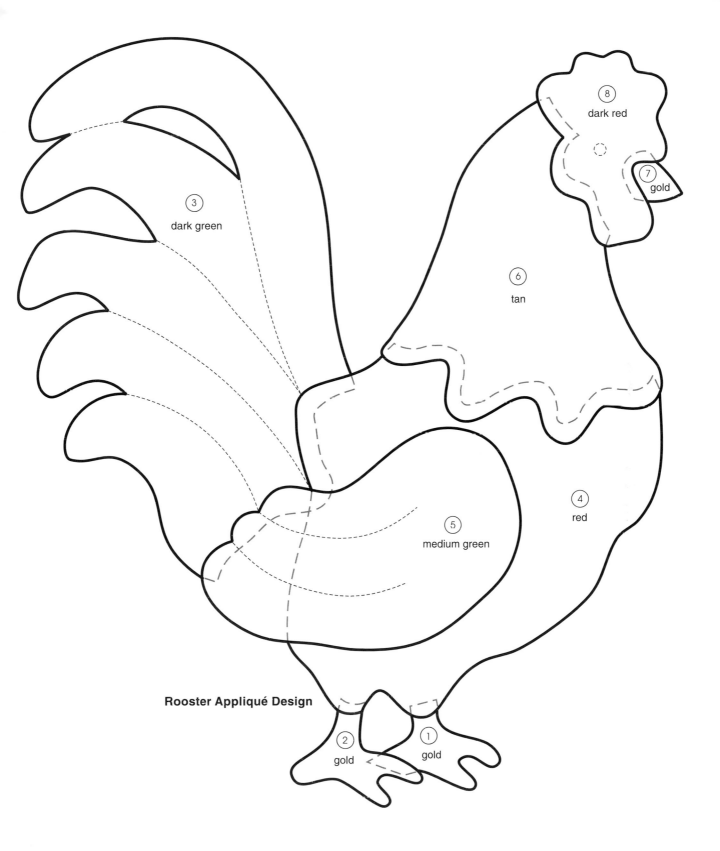

Rooster Appliqué Design

3 dark green

8 dark red

7 gold

6 tan

4 red

5 medium green

2 gold

1 gold

STAINED GLASS CIRCLES

Design by Sue Harvey & Sandy Boobar

There's no curved piecing needed to create the units in this quick-to-piece runner.

PROJECT SPECIFICATIONS

Skill Level: Intermediate

Runner Size: 44" x 26"

SUPPLIES

- Batting 50" x 32"
- Neutral color and black all-purpose thread
- Quilting thread
- 1⅛ yards fabric stabilizer
- Heat-resistant template material
- Spray starch
- Small brush or cotton swab
- Basic tools and supplies

FABRIC Measurements based on 42" usable fabric width.	#STRIPS/ PIECES	CUT	#PIECES	SUBCUT
⅔ yard medium plum tonal	3	5" x 42"	20	5" A squares
	1	9½" x 42"	6	5" B rectangles
⅞ yard black solid	3	4" x 42"	16	4" C squares
			6	8" D rectangles
	1	4¾" E square		
	2	1½" x 36½" I		
	2	1½" x 20½" J		
	4	2¼" x 42" binding		
⅞ yard floral	3	4" x 42"	16	4" F squares
			6	7½" G rectangles
	1	4⅜" H square		
	2	3½" x 38½" K		
	2	3½" x 26½" L		
Backing		50" x 32"		

PREPARING PIECES

Step 1. Prepare a heat-resistant template for the C and F quarter-circles, and D and G half-circles using patterns given.

Step 2. Cut one 4¼" E square and one 3⅞" H square from heat-resistant template material.

Step 3. Center and mark the curved edge of a D half-circle on the wrong side of each D rectangle, aligning the straight edge of the template with one long edge of each rectangle.

Step 4. Cut out the D half-circles, leaving approximately ¼" beyond the marked line as shown in Figure 1.

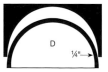

Figure 1

Step 5. Spray a bit of starch into the can's cover or a small dish. Use the small brush or cotton swab to saturate the seam allowance on the curved edge only of one D shape (see page 67).

Step 6. Place the template over the marked shape.

Step 7. Using a hot, dry iron, press the seam allowance

over the edge of the template until dry as shown in Figure 2; repeat with all D shapes.

Figure 2

Step 8. Repeat Steps 2–7 to complete the C, E, F, G and H shapes, aligning both straight edges of the C and F templates on the fabric squares and placing the E and H square templates in the center of the fabric squares to turn under all edges of the E and H squares.

COMPLETING THE UNITS

Step 1. Cut (17) 4¾" squares and six 4¾" x 9" rectangles fabric stabilizer.

Step 2. Place a stabilizer square on the wrong side of an A square.

Step 3. Place a C shape on the A square with corners aligned; place an F shape on the C shape with corners aligned as shown in Figure 3; pin through all layers to hold.

Figure 3   **Figure 4**

Step 4. Stitch along the curved edge of the C shape using black thread and a straight stitch as shown in Figure 4; stitch along the curved edge of the F shape with black thread and a buttonhole or decorative stitch to complete one F unit. Repeat to complete 16 F units; remove fabric stabilizer.

Step 5. Repeat Steps 2–4 with B, D and G rectangles to complete six G units as shown in Figure 5.

Figure 5

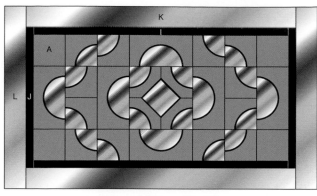

Stained Glass Circles
Placement Diagram 44" x 26"

COMPLETING THE PIECED CENTER

Step 1. Join four F units as shown in Figure 6; press seams in opposite directions.

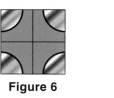

Figure 6   **Figure 7**

Step 2. Center the remaining stabilizer square diagonally on the wrong side of the pieced unit.

Step 3. Center the E square diagonally on the pieced unit with the corners of the square aligning with the seam lines of the pieced unit as shown in Figure 7.

Step 4. Center the H square on the E square; pin in place through all layers.

Step 5. Stitch in place as for the F and G units; remove fabric stabilizer.

Step 6. Join the F and G units in rows with the remaining A squares as shown in Figure 8; press seams in rows in opposite directions.

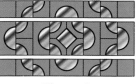

Figure 8

Step 7. Join the rows to complete the pieced center referring to the Placement Diagram for positioning; press seams in one direction.

COMPLETING THE RUNNER

Step 1. Sew I to opposite long sides and J to the short ends of the pieced center; press seams toward I and J.

Step 2. Sew K to opposite long sides and L to the short ends of the pieced center; press seams toward K and L to complete the top.

Step 3. Layer, quilt, prepare binding and bind referring to Completing Your Quilt on page 170. ■

USING SPRAY STARCH ON THE TURNED EDGES OF APPLIQUÉ PIECES

If you are turning under the edges of your appliqué pieces to stitch in place by hand or machine, spray starch helps to keep the edges stiff enough to turn under.

Step 1. Place a piece of freezer paper or parchment paper on a flat surface with a small container or the cover to the spray-starch can.

Step 2. Use a Q-tip or brush to cover the edges of the appliqué pieces.

Step 3. If using heat-resistant template material, after applying the spray starch to the edges, place the template on the wrong side of the piece inside the marked seam allowance. Use the tip of the iron to press the starched seam over onto the template material; remove template after pressing.

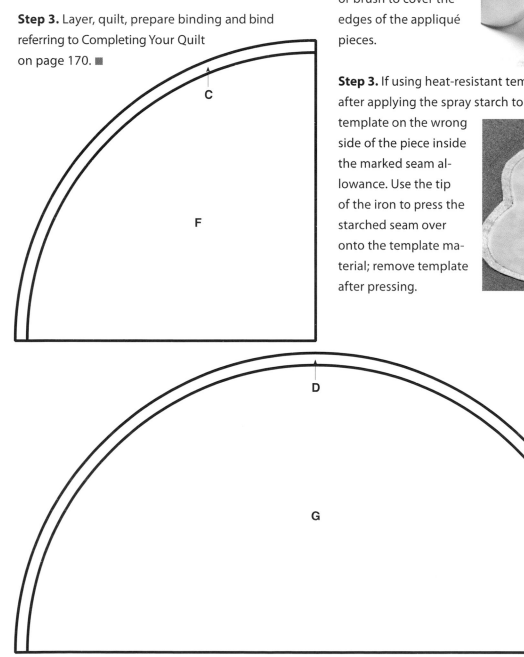

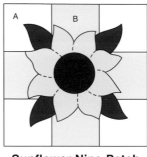

Sunflower Nine-Patch
6" x 6" Block
Make 3

SUNFLOWER TABLE RUNNER

Design by Barbara A. Clayton

Liven up your summertime table settings with this pretty appliquéd and pieced runner.

PROJECT SPECIFICATIONS

Skill Level: Beginner
Runner Size: 28½" x 12½"
Block Size: 6" x 6"
Number of Blocks: 3

SUPPLIES

- Batting 34" x 18"
- All-purpose thread to match fabrics
- Quilting thread
- Clear nylon monofilament
- ¼ yard fusible web
- ¼ yard fabric stabilizer
- Basting spray
- Basic sewing tools and supplies

COMPLETING THE BLOCKS

Step 1. Sew the 16" B strip between the two 16" A strips; press seams toward A.

Step 2. Subcut the A-B-A strip set into six 2½" A-B-A units as shown in Figure 1.

FABRIC Measurements based on 42" usable fabric width.	#STRIPS/PIECES	CUT	#PIECES	SUBCUT
■ Scrap brown tonal		Appliqué pieces as per patterns		
■ Scraps coordinating red, yellow, blue and green prints and florals	38	2½" C squares		
■ ⅛ yard navy/black print	2 2	1¾" x 10½" D 1¾" x 29" E		
□ ⅛ yard yellow tonal		Appliqué pieces as per patterns		
■ ⅛ yard dark green tonal		Appliqué pieces as per patterns		
□ ⅛ yard tan tonal	1	2½" x 42" B	1 2	16" strip 9" strips
□ ⅛ yard cream tonal	1	2½" x 42" A	2 1	16" strips 9" strip
■ ¼ yard red print	3	2¼" x 42" binding		
□ Backing		34" x 18"		

Step 3. Repeat Steps 1 and 2 with the 9" lengths to make a B-A-B strip set; subcut into three 2½" B-A-B units, again referring to Figure 1.

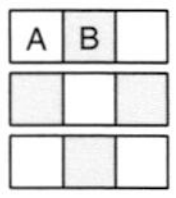

Step 4. Sew a B-A-B unit between two A-B-A units to complete a Nine-Patch unit as shown in Figure 2; press seams in one direction. Repeat to make three Nine-Patch Units.

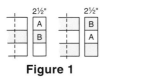

Figure 1

Figure 2

Step 5. Trace the sunflower, center and leaf shapes onto the paper side of the fusible web referring to the patterns for number to cut. Cut out shapes, leaving a margin around each one.

Step 6. Fuse paper shapes to the wrong side of fabrics as directed on patterns for color and number to cut; cut out shapes on traced lines. Remove paper patterns.

Step 7. Center and fuse one sunflower motif, including center and four leaves, to the center of one Nine-Patch unit, tucking leaf shapes under the sunflower shape referring to pattern. Repeat on the remaining Nine-Patch units.

Step 8. Cut three 6" x 6" squares stabilizer; spray-baste a square to the wrong side of each fused Nine-Patch unit.

Step 9. Using thread to match fabrics, stitch on all detail lines and around edges of each shape with a close machine satin stitch. When stitching is complete, remove fabric stabilizer to complete three Sunflower Nine-Patch blocks.

COMPLETING THE RUNNER

Step 1. Select three C squares; join to make a strip. Press seams in one direction. Repeat to make four C end strips.

Step 2. Join the blocks with the C end strips beginning and ending with a strip; press seams away from the blocks.

Step 3. Select 13 C squares; join in a pleasing order to make a C side strip. Press seams in one direction; repeat to make two C side strips.

Step 4. Sew a C side strip to opposite long sides of the pieced center; press seams toward C side strips.

Step 5. Sew a D strip to opposite short ends and E strips to opposite long sides to complete the pieced runner top; press seams toward D and E strips.

Step 6. Layer, quilt, prepare binding and bind edges referring to the General Instructions to finish. ***Note:*** *Clear nylon monofilament was used to machine-quilt around the appliqué shapes.* ■

Sunflower Table Runner
Placement Diagram 28½" x 12½"

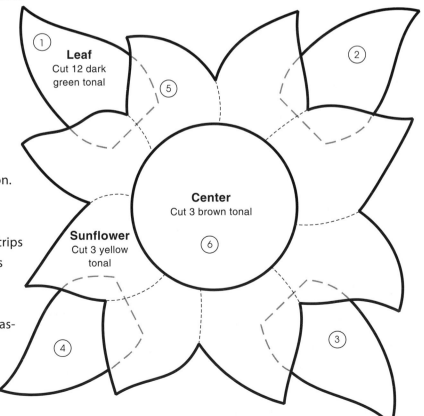

① **Leaf**
Cut 12 dark green tonal
②
⑤

Center
Cut 3 brown tonal
⑥

Sunflower
Cut 3 yellow tonal
④
③

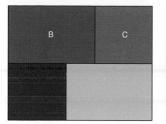

Uneven Four-Patch
5" x 4" Block
Make 4

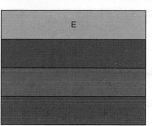

E
5" x 4" Block
Make 1

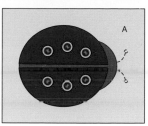

Ladybug
5" x 4" Block
Make 12

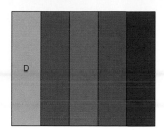

D
5" x 4" Block
Make 1

LADYBUG RUNNER

Design by Nancy Richoux

These little ladies are running in opposite directions on this cute runner.

PROJECT SPECIFICATIONS

Skill Level: Intermediate

Runner Size: 37½" x 15½"

Block Size: 5" x 4"

Number of Blocks: 18

SUPPLIES

- Batting 44" x 22"
- All-purpose thread to match fabrics
- Quilting thread
- Black embroidery floss
- 72 (⅜") black buttons
- Water-soluble marking pen
- Basic tools and supplies

FABRIC Measurements based on 42" usable fabric width.	#STRIPS/ PIECES	CUT	#PIECES	SUBCUT
Assorted red scraps		Appliqué pieces as per pattern		
⅛ yard pale green print	2 2	¾" x 18" G ¾" x 40" H		
⅛ yard black tonal		Appliqué pieces as per pattern		
⅓ yard light green solid	2	4½" x 42"	12	5½" A rectangles
½ yard total dark and medium green prints and tonals	8 8 4 5 4	2½" x 3½" B 2½" x 2½" C 1½" x 12½" F 1½" x 4½" D 1½" x 5½" E		
⅓ yard dark green tonal	2 2	2" x 18" I 2" x 40" J		
Backing		44" x 22"		

COMPLETING THE LADYBUG BLOCKS

Step 1. Prepare templates for ladybug pieces using pattern given. Trace shapes onto the right side of fabrics as directed on each piece for number and color; cut out shapes, leaving ⅛"–¼" all around for seam allowance.

Step 2. Turn under the seam allowance on each piece; baste to hold.

Step 3. Arrange one ladybug motif on one A rectangle; hand-stitch in place.

Step 4. Using 3 strands of black embroidery floss, stem-stitch the antennae, adding a French knot at the end of each one to complete one Ladybug block; repeat to make 12 blocks.

COMPLETING THE D & E BLOCKS

Step 1. Join five D rectangles along the 4½" sides to complete one D block; press seams in one direction.

Step 2. Join four E rectangles along the 5½" sides to complete one E block; press seams in one direction.

COMPLETING THE UNEVEN FOUR-PATCH BLOCKS

Step 1. Sew B to C on the short ends; repeat to make eight B-C units. Press seams toward B.

Step 2. Join two B-C units referring to the block drawing to complete one Uneven Four-Patch block; press seam in one direction. Repeat to make four blocks.

COMPLETING THE RUNNER

Step 1. Arrange and join the Ladybug, D, E and Uneven Four-Patch blocks in three rows referring to the Placement Diagram for positioning of blocks; press seams in adjacent rows in opposite directions.

Step 2. Join the rows to complete the pieced center; press seams in one direction.

Step 3. Join one each dark and medium F strip along length; press seam in one direction. Repeat to make two F units.

Step 4. Sew an F unit to opposite short ends of the pieced center; press seams toward F unit.

Step 5. Sew G to I and H to J along the length; press seams toward I and J. Repeat to make two each G-I and H-J strips.

Step 6. Center and sew a G-I strip to each short end and an H-J strip to opposite long sides of the pieced center, stopping stitching ¼" from ends of the pieced center.

Step 7. Miter corner seams (see page 31), trim seams to ¼" and press open to complete the pieced top.

Step 8. Mark the top for quilting. **Note:** *The sample was hand-quilted in a 1" diagonal grid through the center area, in the ditch of seams and in straight lines on the borders.*

Step 9. Lay the backing wrong side up on a flat surface; place batting on top. Center the completed top right side up on the batting.

Step 10. Quilt on the marked lines or as desired.

Step 11. Trim batting even with quilted top; trim backing ⅝" wider than top all around. Press under ¼" on all sides of the backing piece. Bring the excess backing to the right side and hand-stitch in place on the outside border strips.

Step 12. Hand-stitch six buttons on each ladybug referring to patterns for placement to finish. ■

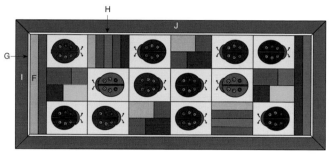

Ladybug Runner
Placement Diagram 37½" x 15½"

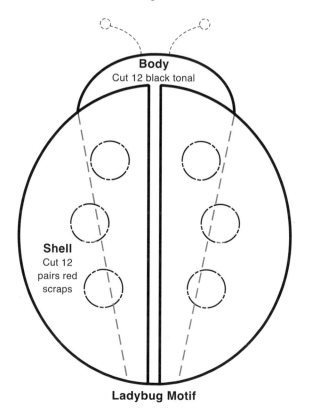

Ladybug Motif

THERE'S MORE THAN ONE WAY TO CUT A QUILT

Ready to try something new? Here are several different approaches to creating the pieces for a quilt. Try cutting a stack of fat quarters, all at the same time. Use cookie cutters or a die-cut machine to create special shapes. Or use card stock and try your hand at English paper piecing.

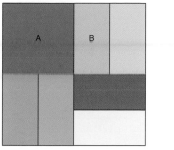

Spring Fling Pillow
Placement Diagram 16" x 16"

20/20
SPRING FLING

Designs by Karen Blocher

With 20 fat quarters and 20 slices of a rotary cutter, the top of this quilt is ready for assembly and can be pieced together in just a few hours.

PROJECT SPECIFICATIONS

Skill Level: Beginner
Quilt Size: 80" x 96"
Pillow Size: 16" x 16"

SUPPLIES

- Batting 86" x 102" for quilt and 4 (16½") squares for pillows
- All-purpose thread to match fabrics
- Quilting thread
- 4 (16") pillow forms
- Basic sewing tools and supplies

COMPLETING THE QUILT

Step 1. Press and square the left side and top of all 20 fat quarters; stack and align five fat quarters with long sides at the top. Cut the stack as shown in Figure 1 to make four 8½" x 8½" A squares and two 4½" x 8½" B rectangles of each fabric. Repeat with all fat quarters.

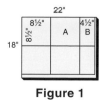

Figure 1

Step 2. Select and join 10 A squares to make an A row; press seams in one direction. Repeat to make

FABRIC Measurements based on 42" usable fabric width.	#STRIPS/ PIECES	CUT
20 assorted fat quarters		
1⅛ yards pillow backing fabric	8	11" x 16½" rectangles
2⅔ yards coordinating print	8	8½" x 42" C
	9	2¼" x 42" binding
Backing		86" x 102"

four A rows. ***Note:** The squares may be arranged randomly or in a planned order.*

Step 3. Select and join nine A squares and add a B rectangle on each end to make a B row; press seams in one direction. Repeat to make four B rows.

Step 4. Join the A and B rows, alternating rows, to complete the pieced center; press seams in one direction.

Step 5. Join the C strips with right sides together on the short ends to make one long strip; press seams open. Subcut the strip into four 80½" C strips.

Step 6. Sew a C strip to opposite sides and then to the top and bottom of the pieced center; press seams toward C strips to complete the pieced top.

Step 7. Layer, quilt, prepare binding and bind edges referring to the General Instructions.

COMPLETING THE PILLOW

Step 1. Join two B rectangles along the 8½" sides to make a B unit; press seam in one direction. Repeat to make 12 B units.

Step 2. To complete one pillow top, join two B units to make a row as shown in Figure 2; press seams in one direction.

Figure 2

Step 3. Sew a B unit to A to make a second row, again referring to Figure 2; press seam toward A.

Step 4. Join the rows to complete one pillow top referring to the Placement Diagram; press seam in one direction. Repeat to make four pillow tops.

Step 5. Place a pillow top on a batting square; quilt as desired.

Step 6. Turn under one 16½" edge of each backing piece ¼"; press. Turn under again ½"; press and stitch to hem.

Step 7. Place one hemmed backing piece right sides together with one pillow top, matching raw edges as shown in Figure 3; pin to hold. Repeat with a second hemmed backing piece, overlapping hemmed edges as shown in Figure 4; baste to hold.

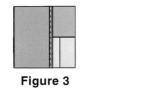

Figure 3

Figure 4

Step 8. Stitch layers together all around; clip corners and turn right side out. Press edges flat; insert pillow form to finish. Repeat to make four pillows. ■

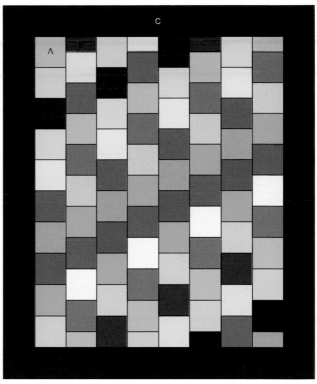

20/20 Spring Fling
Placement Diagram 80" x 96"

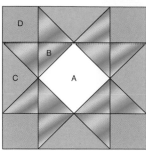

Star Flower
12" x 12" Block
Make 18

BLOOMING FLOWERS

Design by Sandra L. Hatch

Flower power is at its best in this bright-colored quilt.

PROJECT SPECIFICATIONS
Skill Level: Beginner
Quilt Size: 78" x 90"
Block Size: 12" x 12"
Number of Blocks: 18

SUPPLIES
- Batting 84" x 96"
- All-purpose thread to match fabrics
- Quilting thread
- 1 yard lightweight fusible web
- Basic sewing tools and supplies

FABRIC Measurements based on 42" usable fabric width.	#STRIPS/ PIECES	CUT	#PIECES	SUBCUT
1 yard dark pink tonal dot	9	2¼" x 43" binding Appliqué pieces as per pattern		
1 yard pink floral	6	3½" x 43" Appliqué pieces as per instructions	72	3½" D squares
1¼ yards orange tonal	6	6½" x 43"	72	3½" C rectangles
1⅞ yards white dot	3	6½" x 43"	18	6½" A squares
	4	7" x 42½" E		
	7	1½" x 43" H/I		
4½ yards multicolored print	18	3½" x 43"	216	3½" B squares
	5	2½" x 42½" F		
	2	3½" x 36½" G		
	8	8½" x 43" J/K		
Backing		84" x 96"		

COMPLETING THE BLOCKS

Step 1. Mark a diagonal line from corner to corner on the wrong side of each B square.

Step 2. Referring to Figure 1, place B on opposite corners of A and stitch on the marked lines; trim seams to ¼" and press B to the right side.

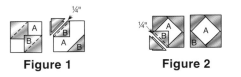

Figure 1   **Figure 2**

Step 3. Repeat Step 2 to complete an A-B unit referring to Figure 2; repeat to make 18 A-B units.

Step 4. Repeat Step 2 with B on each end of C to complete a B-C unit as shown in Figure 3; repeat to make 72 B-C units.

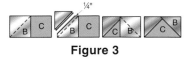

Figure 3

Step 5. To complete one Star Flower block, sew a B-C unit to opposite sides of an A-B unit to make a center row as shown in Figure 4; press seams toward the A-B unit.

Figure 4

Step 6. Sew D to each end of two B-C units to make two B-C-D units as shown in Figure 5; press seams toward D.

Figure 5

Step 7. Sew the B-C-D units to opposite sides of the center row referring to the block drawing to complete one Star Flower block; press seams away from the center row. Repeat to make 18 blocks.

COMPLETING THE QUILT

Step 1. Join four E strips with five F strips; press seams toward F.

Step 2. Add G to the top and bottom of the E-F panel to complete the pieced center.

Step 3. Join four Star Flower blocks to make a side row; press seams in one direction. Repeat to make two side rows.

Step 4. Sew a side row to opposite sides of the pieced center; press seams away from the side rows.

Step 5. Join five Star Flower blocks to make the top row; press seams in one direction. Repeat to make the bottom row.

Step 6. Sew the top and bottom rows to the pieced center; press seams toward the top and bottom rows.

Step 7. Join the H/I strips on short ends to make one long strip; press seams open. Subcut strip into two 72½" H strips and two 62½" I strips.

Step 8. Sew the H strips to opposite long sides and I strips to the top and bottom of the pieced center; press seams toward H and I strips.

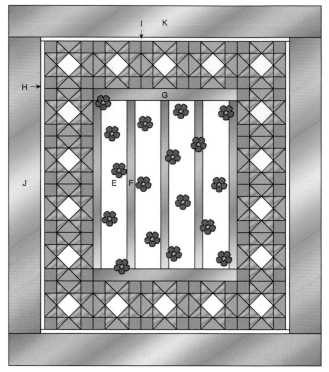

Blooming Flowers
Placement Diagram 78" x 90"

Step 9. Join the J/K strips on short ends to make one long strip; press seams open. Subcut strip into two 74½" J strips and two 78½" K strips.

Step 10. Sew the J strips to opposite sides and K strips to the top and bottom of the pieced center; press seams toward J and K strips.

Step 11. Cut two 6" x 18" pieces fusible web; bond to the wrong side of the pink floral. Cut out 17 small printed floral designs for flower centers; remove paper backing.

Step 12. Trace 17 flower shapes onto the paper side of the fusible web. Cut out shapes, leaving a margin around each one; fuse shapes to the wrong side of the dark pink tonal dot. Cut out shapes on traced lines.

Step 13. Center a small printed flower on a large cutout flower; fuse in place. Repeat for all flowers.

Step 14. Remove paper backing from the large flowers. Randomly arrange and fuse the flowers over the pieced center area referring to the Placement Diagram and quilt photo for suggestions.

Step 15. Layer, quilt, prepare binding and bind edges referring to the General Instructions. ***Note:*** *The flower shapes are held in place with quilting; they are not stitched in place separately. Edges will fray with washings.* ■

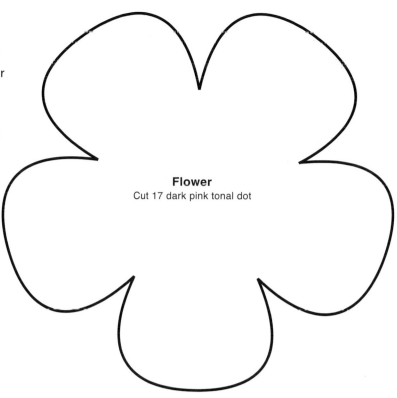

Flower
Cut 17 dark pink tonal dot

USING DIE-CUTTERS

A die-cutting machine makes short work of cutting appliqué shapes of consistent size. Your local quilt shop may have one of these machines. Refer to the following instructions for use.

Step 1. Bond fusible web to the wrong side of the fabric from which flowers will be cut to cover a 9" by fabric width area.

Step 2. Cut the fused fabric into two 4" by fabric width strips; subcut strips into (17) 4" squares.

Step 3. Stack four fused squares together and cut using the die-cutting machine with a flower die; continue cutting until all flowers are cut.

Step 4. Use the cut flowers as per instructions in Completing the Quilt.

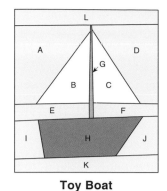

Toy Boat
7" x 8" Block
Make 20

TOY BOAT REGATTA

Design by Jodi G. Warner

Use the stack-and-slash construction method to create the blocks for this scrappy quilt.

PROJECT SPECIFICATIONS

Skill Level: Advanced

Quilt Size: 45" x 58½"

Block Size: 7" x 8"

Number of Blocks: 20

SUPPLIES

- Batting 51" x 64"
- All-purpose thread to match fabrics
- Quilting thread
- Basic sewing tools and supplies

CUTTING USING DIAGRAMS

Step 1. Make copies of Diagrams 1–6 as directed on patterns.

Step 2. Trim each copy ⅛" beyond the outer solid cutting line.

Step 3. Position and pin (one pin in each division, placed away from cutting lines) each trimmed diagram on top of neatly stacked and smoothed layers of designated fabrics, which are all right side up.

Step 4. First, cut around outside lines, then follow cutting instructions on diagrams for order.

FABRIC Measurements based on 42" usable fabric width.	#STRIPS/PIECES	CUT	#PIECES	SUBCUT
☐ 10 fat eighths aqua green for background	2	1¾" x 8" L each fabric A, D, E, F, I, J, K pieces as per patterns		
☐ Scraps	2	6" x 8" rectangles each 5 different black–on–white prints for B and C sails		
	1	5" x 12" H rectangle each 5 different coordinated brights for ship hulls		
	1	4" x 6" G rectangle each 5 different browns for ship masts		
■ ⅛ yard navy plaid	2	2" x 42"	30	2" N squares
☐ ¼ yard lime green tonal	2 3	1¼" x 37½" Q 1¼" x 42" P		
☐ ¾ yard cream/aqua print	5	4½" x 42" R/S		
☐ 1½ yards dark aqua check	2 2 6	7½" x 42" 8½" x 42" 2¼" x 42" binding	24 25	2" M rectangles 2" O rectangles
☐ Backing		51" x 64"		

Step 5. After the first or second, etc., cuts are completed, make remaining cuts to subdivide separated sections; no order is necessary for these cuts.

Step 6. Discard any sections marked on diagrams with X's.

Step 7. Place same-fabric pieces in stacks; arrange in block layout for ease in piecing.

COMPLETING THE BLOCKS

Notes: For ease in piecing, keep stacks of same-fabric pieces in order with the following exception: Take the top C sail triangle and place on the bottom of the stack so that same-fabric B and C sails will not be stitched into one block. Since blocks will be trimmed to size after piecing is complete, all edges will not align during piecing. Background fabric within each block should match.

Step 1. Sew A to B and C to D as shown in Figure 1; press seams toward B or C. Repeat to make 20 each A-B and C-D units.

Figure 1

Figure 2

Step 2. Sew E to the bottom edge of each A-B unit and F to the bottom edges of C-D units, aligning one end of E or F with the edge of B or C as shown in Figure 2; press seams toward E or F.

Step 3. Sew G to the B edge of each A-B-E unit, aligning lower edges as shown in Figure 3; press seams toward G.

Figure 3   **Figure 4**

Step 4. Sew the F/C edge to the G edge, aligning E and F seams across G as closely as possible, referring to the block drawing; press seams toward F/C.

Step 5. Sew I to the left edge and J to the right edge of H, aligning upper edges of all pieces as shown in Figure 4.

Step 6. Using a rotary cutter and straightedge, trim excess I and J even with lower H edge referring to Figure 5.

Figure 5   **Figure 6**

Step 7. Sew the I-H-J unit to the sail unit, matching the I-H seam to the A-B seam and the H-J seam to the C-D seam across the E and F strips referring to the block drawing.

Step 8. Center and sew K to the bottom and L to the top of each block as shown in Figure 6; press seams toward K and L strips.

Step 9. Trim blocks to 7½" x 8½".

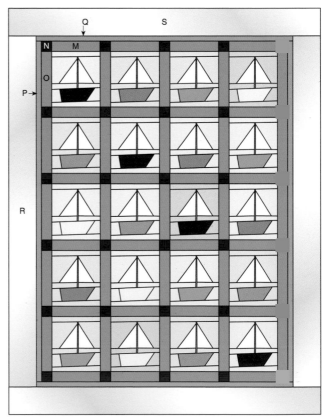

Toy Boat Regatta
Placement Diagram 45" x 58½"

COMPLETING THE QUILT

Step 1. Arrange blocks, alternating background fabrics, to make five rows of four blocks each.

Step 2. Join four blocks as arranged with five O strips to make a block row; press seams toward O strips. Repeat to make five block rows.

Step 3. Join four M strips with five N squares to make a sashing row; press seams toward M strips. Repeat to make six sashing rows.

Step 4. Join the block rows as arranged with the sashing rows to complete the pieced center; press seams toward sashing rows.

Step 5. Join P strips on short ends to make one long strip; press seams open. Subcut strip into two 49½" P strips.

Step 6. Sew P strips to opposite long sides and Q strips to the top and bottom of the pieced center; press seams toward P and Q strips.

Step 7. Join the R/S strips on short ends to make one long strip; press seams open. Subcut strip into two 51" R and two 45½" S strips.

Step 8. Sew R strips to opposite long sides and S strips to the top and bottom of the pieced center; press seams toward R and S strips.

Step 9. Layer, quilt, prepare binding and bind edges referring to the General Instructions. ■

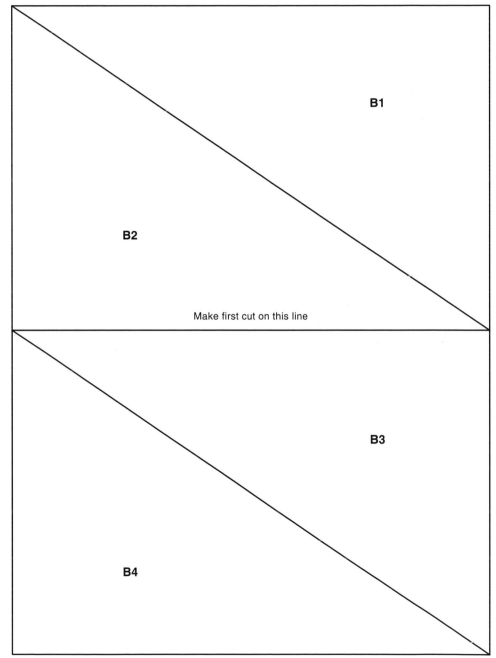

Diagram 3 – White Sail
Make 1 copy
Place this diagram on top of 5 layers of white sail fabrics, all right side up.

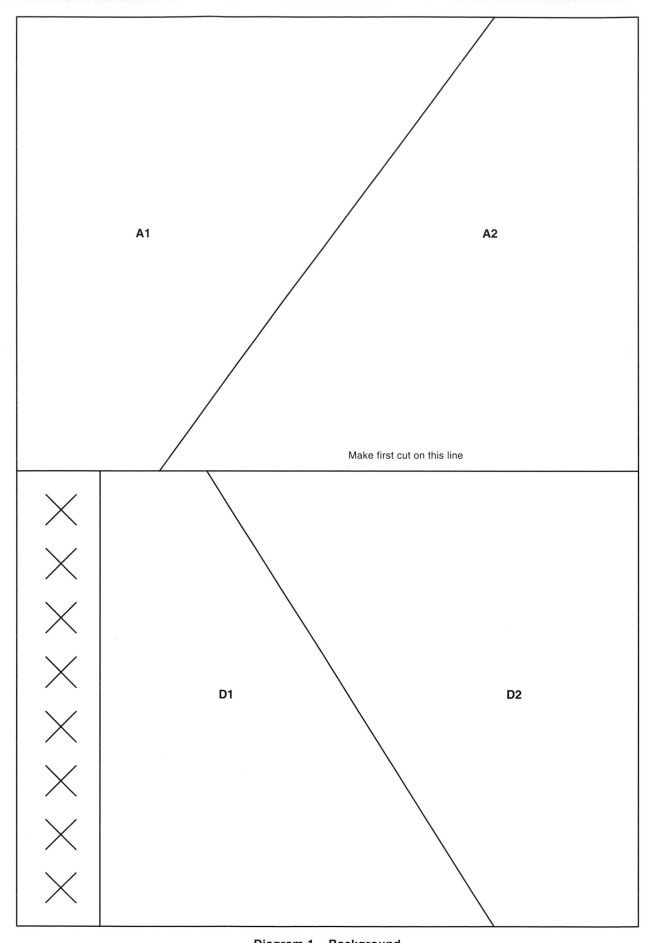

Diagram 1 – Background
Make 2 copies
Place 1 copy on top of 5 layers of background fabrics, all right side up. Repeat with second copy on 5 remaining background fabrics.

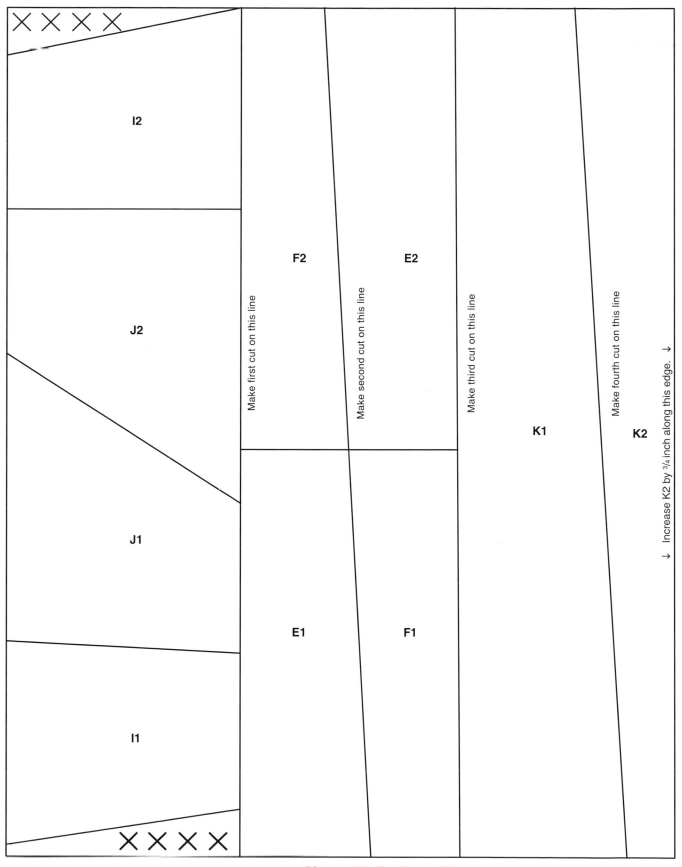

Diagram 2 – Background
Make 2 copies
Place 1 copy on top of 5 layers of background fabrics, all right side up. Repeat with second copy on 5 remaining background fabrics.

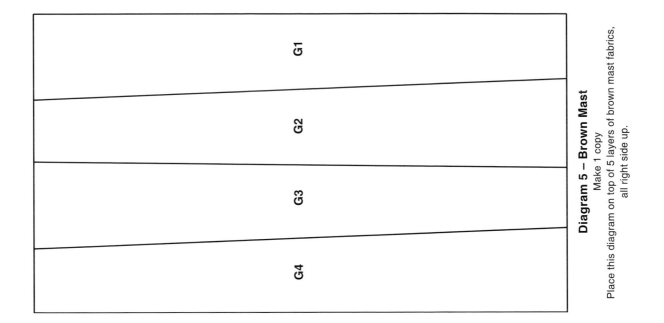

Diagram 5 – Brown Mast
Make 1 copy
Place this diagram on top of 5 layers of brown mast fabrics, all right side up.

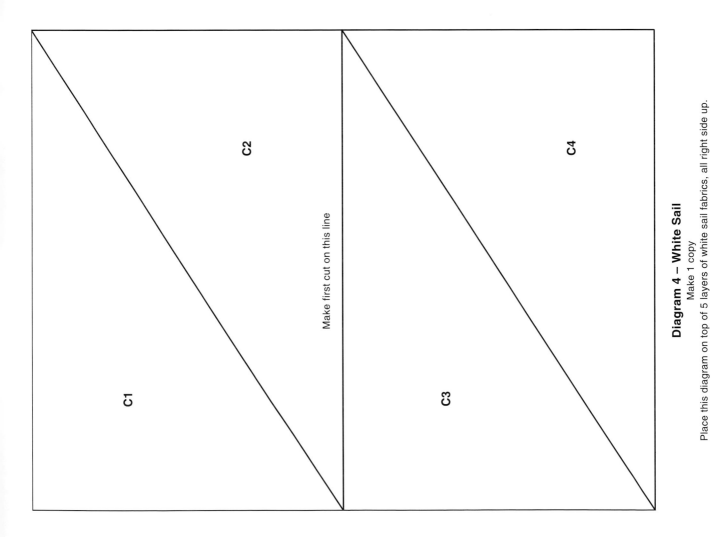

Diagram 4 – White Sail
Make 1 copy
Place this diagram on top of 5 layers of white sail fabrics, all right side up.

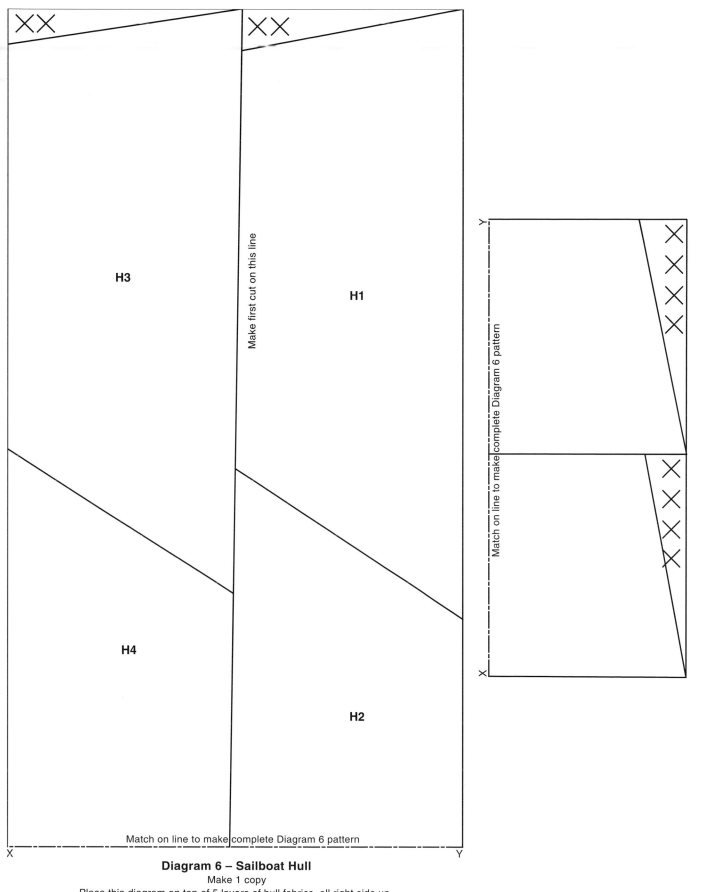

Diagram 6 – Sailboat Hull
Make 1 copy
Place this diagram on top of 5 layers of hull fabrics, all right side up.

Cookie-Cutter Crazy
7½" x 7½" Block
Make 5

COOKIE-CUTTER CRAZY

Design by Sandra L. Hatch

Gather the children and make a cookie-cutter crazy quilt instead of cookies.

PROJECT NOTES

There is no planned arrangement of these fabrics in the sample quilt. If desired, each square can be of a different fabric.

PROJECT SPECIFICATIONS

Skill Level: Beginner
Quilt Size: 69½" x 87½"
Block Size: 7½" x 7½"
Number of Blocks: 5

SUPPLIES

- Batting 76" x 94"
- Multicolor matching thread
- 1 yard fusible web
- ¾ yard fabric stabilizer
- Christmas cookie cutters
- Basic sewing tools and supplies

COOKIE-CUTTER CRAZY APPLIQUÉ

Step 1. Cut eight 9" x 8" rectangles fusible web; fuse rectangles to the wrong side of the remainder of the fabrics used for A squares.

Step 2. Select cookie cutters and trace onto the paper side of the fused fabrics. You will need two or three shapes per block depending on the size of the cutters.

Step 3. Cut out traced shapes and cut other free-form shapes from the fused fabrics; remove paper backing.

FABRIC Measurements based on 42" usable fabric width.	#STRIPS/ PIECES	CUT
4 (8") D squares holiday preprint		
¼ yard each 8 different fabrics in green, burgundy, cream and multicolor prints or tonals	31	8" A squares total
¼ yard cream tonal	5	8" C squares
½ yard cream print	7	1½" x 42" G/H strips
2½ yards Christmas print	2	6½" x 76" I along length of fabric
	5	8" B squares
	5	6½" J by remaining fabric width
2⅝ yards burgundy tonal	6	3½" x 68" E along length of fabric
	2	3½" x 56" F along length of fabric
	8	2¼" x 42" binding
Backing		76" x 94"

Step 4. Arrange shapes on the C squares, leaving ½" all around outside and small spaces between shapes referring to Figure 1; when satisfied with arrangement, fuse shapes in place.

Figure 1

Step 5. Cut five 8" x 8" squares fabric stabilizer and pin to the wrong side of each fused C square.

Step 6. Machine zigzag-stitch around each fused shape to complete the blocks. When stitching is complete, remove fabric stabilizer.

COMPLETING THE QUILT

Step 1. Arrange the blocks with the A, B and D squares in five rows of nine squares each referring to the Placement Diagram for positioning of squares; press seams in one direction.

Step 2. Join the rows with the E strips; press seams toward E.

Step 3. Sew an F strip to the top and bottom of the pieced center; press seams toward F.

Step 4. Join the G/H strips on short ends to make one long strip; press seams open. Subcut strip into two 74" G strips and two 58" H strips.

Step 5. Sew G strips to opposite sides and H strips to the top and bottom of the pieced center; press seams toward G and H.

Step 6. Join the J strips on short ends to make one long strip; press seams open. Subcut two 70" J strips from the pieced strip.

Step 7. Sew an I strip to opposite long sides and J to the top and bottom of the pieced center; press seams toward I and J to complete the top. *Note: The fabric used was a directional print. If you are using a directional print, try to join the strips so that the design flows and the seam is not obvious. If your fabric is not a directional print, cut two 6½" x 70" strips along the length of the fabric.*

Step 8. Layer, quilt, prepare binding and bind edges referring to the General Instructions. ■

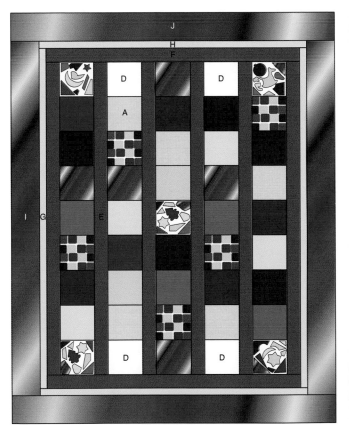

Cookie-Cutter Crazy
Placement Diagram 69½" x 87½"

THE ONLY THING BETTER THAN A QUILT IS A QUILT WITH ACCESSORIES

The trend in home decorating today is to add lots of accessories. Whether you choose to make some pillows or to embellish sheets to match your quilt, you will find the added touch creates a comfortable mood for your room.

2-Leaf Flower 1
8" x 8" Block
Make 16 red, 13 gold,
9 navy & 4 blue

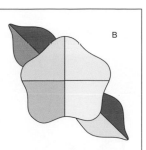

2-Leaf Flower 2
8" x 8" Block
Make 7 gold, 2 red & 1 blue

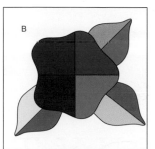

3-Leaf Flower
8" x 8" Block
Make 6 blue, 4 red,
2 gold & 2 navy

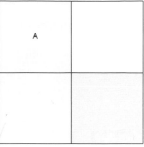

Four-Patch
8" x 8" Block
Make 66

PATCHWORK POSIES

Designs by Chris Malone

Coordinate your bedroom's decor with a quilt,
runner, sheet and pillowcases.

PROJECT SPECIFICATIONS

Skill Level: Advanced

Quilt Size: 88" x 96"

Runner Size: 30" x 12"

Block Size: 8" x 8"

Number of Blocks: 132

SUPPLIES

- Batting 94" x 102" for quilt and 30½" x 12½"
  for runner
- 10 (3½" x 4") rectangles batting for runner leaves
- All-purpose thread to match fabrics
- Machine-embroidery thread to match
  appliqué fabrics
- Quilting thread
- 3½ yards 18"-wide lightweight fusible web
- 8 (⅝") white pearl buttons
- 10 (⅞") white pearl buttons
- Fray preventative (optional)
- 1 purchased ivory flat sheet (model is full-size)
- 2 purchased standard-size ivory pillowcases
- Basic sewing tools and supplies

COMPLETING THE FLOWER BLOCKS

Step 1. Join two C strips with right sides together
along length to make a C strip set; press seam toward

FABRIC Measurements based on 42" usable fabric width.	#STRIPS/ PIECES	CUT	#PIECES	SUBCUT
⅔ yard total navy prints and tonals	4	Appliqué pieces as per patterns 3½" x 42" F		
⅔ yard total blue prints and tonals	4	Appliqué pieces as per patterns 3½" x 42" D		
⅔ yard lining fabric	4	4¾" x 22½"		
1 yard total 3 dark green tonals	6 13	Appliqué pieces as per patterns 3½" x 8" leaf rectangles 1¾" x 42" J		
1 yard total 3 light green tonals	4 13	Appliqué pieces as per patterns 3½" x 8" leaf rectangles 1¾" x 42" K		
1 yard total red prints and tonals	8	Appliqué pieces as per patterns 3½" x 42" E		
1 yard total gold prints and tonals	8	Appliqué pieces as per patterns 3½" x 42" C		
10 yards total cream/tan tonals prints and stripes	30 17 24 2 22 10	4½" x 42" A 8½" x 42" 3½" G squares 6½" x 12½" H rectangles one fabric 4½" I squares 2¼" x 42"	66 20	8½" B squares 21" binding strips
Backing		94" x 102" for quilt 39½" x 12½ for runner		

darker fabric. Repeat to make four each C and E, and two each D and F strip sets.

Step 2. Subcut strip sets into 3½" segments as follows and referring to Figure 1: 46 each C and E, and 24 each D and F.

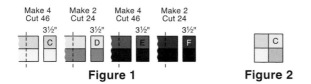

Figure 1

Figure 2

Step 3. Join two C segments as shown in Figure 2; press seam in one direction. Repeat for all C, D, E and F segments.

Step 4. Trace large flower and large leaf shapes onto the paper side of the lightweight fusible web referring to patterns for number to cut and transferring dashed lines on pattern to the paper side of the shapes; cut out shapes, leaving a margin around each one.

Step 5. Repeat Step 1 with J and K strips to complete 13 J/K strip sets.

Step 6. Fuse flower shapes to the wrong side of the joined C, D, E and F units, aligning marked lines on paper to seams on the joined units as shown in Figure 3; cut out shapes. Remove paper backing. Set aside one each C, D, E and F unit for runner.

Figure 3

Step 7. Referring to the pattern, fuse leaf shapes onto the wrong side of the J/K strip sets, aligning the marked centerline on the paper with the seam on the strip sets; cut out shapes on traced lines. Remove paper backing.

Step 8. Fold and crease B squares to mark the vertical, horizontal and diagonal centers.

Step 9. Arrange J-K leaf and C, D, E and F flower units on B squares referring to the block drawings, tuck-

ing the end of the leaf shapes under the edge of the flower shapes before fusing shapes in place.

Step 10. Using machine-embroidery thread to match flower fabric, machine-appliqué around edges of each shape using a machine blanket stitch to complete the Flower blocks.

COMPLETING THE FOUR-PATCH BLOCKS

Step 1. Join two A strips with right sides together along length to make an A strip set; press seam in one direction. Repeat to make 15 A strip sets.

Step 2. Subcut the A strip sets into (132) 4½" A units as shown in Figure 4.

Figure 4   **Figure 5**

Step 3. Join two A units as shown in Figure 5 to complete a Four-Patch block; press seam in one direction. Repeat to make 66 Four-Patch blocks.

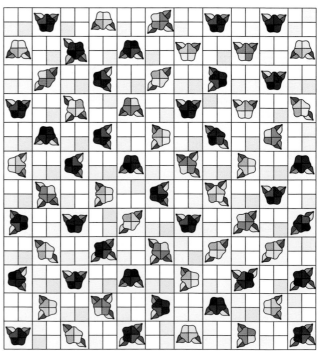

Patchwork Posies
Placement Diagram 88" x 96"

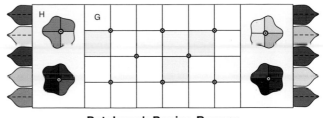

Patchwork Posies Runner
Placement Diagram 30" x 12"
without leaves

COMPLETING THE QUILT

Step 1. Arrange the Four-Patch blocks with the flower blocks to make 12 rows of 11 blocks each referring to the Placement Diagram for positioning of blocks. Press seams in adjoining rows in opposite directions.

Step 2. Join the rows to complete the pieced top, again referring to the Placement Diagram for positioning of rows; press seams in one direction.

Step 3. Layer, quilt, prepare binding and bind edges referring to the General Instructions.

COMPLETING THE RUNNER

Step 1. Join four G squares to make a G row; press seams in one direction. Repeat to make six G rows.

Step 2. Join the G rows to complete the pieced center; press seams in one direction.

Step 3. Sew an H strip to each end of the pieced center; press seams toward H.

Step 4. Arrange and fuse one each D and E flower on one H, and a C and F flower on the other H referring to the Placement Diagram for positioning.

Step 5. Trace the leaf pattern on one end of the wrong side of one leaf rectangle as shown in Figure 6; fold the leaf rectangle with right sides together and pin to a batting rectangle.

Figure 6

Figure 7

Step 6. Stitch on the marked line through all layers, leaving straight end open; trim batting close to seam, trim seam and clip curves. Turn right side out through opening, smooth and press flat.

Step 7. Topstitch through the center of each leaf as shown in Figure 7. Repeat Steps 5–7 to complete six dark and four light leaves.

Step 8. Arrange and pin three dark and two light leaves to each H end of the pieced top as shown in Figure 8; machine-baste to hold in place.

Figure 8

Step 9. Place the runner backing right sides together with the pieced runner top; place the batting on the bottom. Pin layers to hold; stitch all around, leaving an 8" opening on one side. Trim batting close to seam.

Step 10. Turn runner right side out through opening; press flat. Press opening seam ¼" to the inside and hand-stitch closed.

Step 11. Sew a ⅞" button in the center of each flower and a ⅝" button in the joining seams of the center G squares referring to the Placement Diagram for positioning to finish.

COMPLETING THE APPLIQUÉD SHEET

Step 1. Trace small flower and leaf shapes onto the paper side of the fusible web referring to patterns for number to cut; cut out shapes, leaving a margin all around.

Step 2. Fuse shapes to the wrong side of fabrics as directed on patterns for color and number to cut.

Step 3. Cut out shapes on marked lines; remove paper backing.

Step 4. Fold the sheet to find the center of the top band; pin to mark.

Step 5. Starting 1" from each side of the marked center, arrange and fuse three leaves, one each navy or blue, red and gold flower and three more leaves as shown in Figure 9.

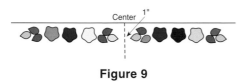

Figure 9

Step 6. Machine-appliqué pieces in place using a blanket stitch and machine-embroidery thread to match fabrics. Add a straight stitch through the center of each leaf.

Step 7. Sew a ⅞" button in the center of each flower to finish.

COMPLETING THE PILLOWCASES

Step 1. Join 11 I squares to make a strip; press seams in one direction. Repeat to make two strips.

Step 2. Cut the hemmed band off each pillowcase and open pillowcase side seam about 2".

Step 3. Sew a pieced I strip to the cut end of each pillowcase; press seam toward the I strip. Trim I strip even with pillowcase edge.

Step 4. Join the lining strips on the short ends to make two 4¾" x 44½" strips. Press a ⅜" hem along one long edge of each strip.

Step 5. Pin and stitch the remaining long raw edge of each lining strip to the I end of each pillowcase.

Step 6. Fold the lining strip to the inside at the seam line and press; pin in place.

Step 7. From the front side, stitch in the seam between the pillowcase and the band, catching the lining hem on the inside as shown in Figure 10.

Figure 10

Step 8. Re-stitch the pillowcase seam opening and edges of band; finish seam edges with a zigzag stitch or serger. ■

SEALING FABRIC EDGES TO PREVENT FRAYING

Fray Check, a commercial fabric-sealing product, is used to keep fabric from fraying and seals thread ends. It can be used on the edges of seams that might ravel or the ends of ribbon or appliqué pieces that will be applied using fusible web.

It will not discolor or stain most fabrics. To guarantee that your fabric will not run when using a sealing product, test a small scrap on a piece of white paper. If the color doesn't run, it is safe to use.

Fray Check is applied with the applicator tip that is part of the purchased bottle.

Small Flower
Cut 2 each gold & red, & 1 each blue & navy for sheet

Small Leaf
Cut 8 dark & 4 light green tonals for sheet

Large Flower
Cut 22 each gold & red, & 11 each navy & blue for quilt
Cut 1 each gold, red, navy & blue for runner

Patchwork Posies Pillowcase Band
Placement Diagram
4" wide

Large Leaf
Cut 146 from J/K strip sets for quilt
Cut 6 dark green pairs & 4 light green pairs for runner
Add ¼" seam allowance on curved sides when cutting for runner.

Handkerchief
12" x 12" Block
Make 20 for quilt
Make 1 for pillow

DAINTY HANDKERCHIEF

Design by Mary Ayers

Make good use of vintage handkerchiefs in this pretty quilt.

QUILT
PROJECT SPECIFICATIONS

Skill Level: Beginner

Quilt Size: 48" x 60" (without trim)

Block Size: 12" x 12"

Number of Blocks: 20

SUPPLIES

- 10 vintage handkerchiefs
- Batting 50" x 62"
- All-purpose thread to match fabrics
- Quilting thread
- 6½ yards crocheted trim
- 10 yards ⅞"-wide pink satin ribbon
- Basic sewing tools and supplies

COMPLETING THE BLOCKS

Step 1. Cut each handkerchief in half on one diagonal.

Step 2. Pin and machine-baste one handkerchief to one side of an A square, moving the handkerchief until the angled edges are even with the corners of the square and the point is centered in the square width as shown

Figure 1

Figure 2

FABRIC Measurements based on 42" usable fabric width.	#STRIPS/ PIECES	CUT
1½ yards pink floral	10	12¾" A squares
1½ yards pink plaid	10	12¾" B squares
Backing		50" x 62"

in Figure 1. ***Note:*** *Not all handkerchiefs will be the same size, so more may be trimmed from some than others.*

Step 3. Trim excess handkerchief even with the edges of A, referring to Figure 2, to complete one block.

Step 4. Hand-stitch the finished edges of the handkerchief to A.

Step 5. Repeat Steps 2–4 with remaining A and B squares to complete 20 Handkerchief blocks.

COMPLETING THE QUILT

Note: *Use a ⅜" seam allowance for all stitching in this project.*

Step 1. Join two each A and B Handkerchief blocks to make an X row, beginning with the A block; press seams toward B blocks. Repeat to make three X rows.

Step 2. Repeat Step 1 beginning with a B block

to make a Y row; press seams toward B block row. Repeat to make two Y blocks.

Step 3. Join the rows referring to the Placement Diagram for positioning; press seams in one direction.

Step 4. Beginning at one corner, baste the straight edge of the crocheted trim around the edges of the pieced top ⅜" from edge, gathering 2½" at each corner; whipstitch ends together.

Step 5. Place the batting on a flat surface with the backing piece right side up on top; place the quilt top on the backing with right sides together, tucking crocheted trim inside. Trim excess batting and backing even with quilt top. Stitch all around, leaving an 8" opening on one side.

Step 6. Trim seams at corners; turn right side out through the opening. Press edges flat.

Step 7. Turn opening edges to the inside ⅜"; press. Hand-stitch opening closed.

Step 8. Cut the ribbon into (20) 18" lengths; tie each length into a bow.

Step 9. Hand-stitch a bow to the point of each hand-kerchief through all layers to complete the quilt. *Note: The stitching that holds the bows in place also holds the layers together. You may stitch in the ditch of seams and as desired to add quilting.*

PILLOW
PROJECT SPECIFICATIONS
Skill Level: Beginner
Pillow Size: 12" x 12"
Block Size: 12" x 12"
Number of Blocks: 1

MATERIALS
- 1 vintage handkerchief
- ⅜ yard pink floral
  1 - 12¾" x 12¾" backing square
- ⅜ yard pink plaid
  1 - 12¾" x 12¾" B square
- Batting 12¾" x 12¾"
- All-purpose thread to match fabrics
- Quilting thread
- 1½ yards pink jumbo rickrack
- ½ yard ⅞"-wide pink satin ribbon
- 12" pillow form
- Basic sewing tools and supplies

COMPLETING THE PILLOW
Note: Use a ⅜" seam allowance for all stitching in this project.

Step 1. With B square, complete one handkerchief block referring to Completing the Blocks for quilt.

Step 2. Tie the ribbon into a bow; hand-stitch the bow on the point of the handkerchief.

Dainty Handkerchief
Placement Diagram 48" x 60" (without trim)

Step 3. Hand-baste the pink jumbo rickrack ⅜" from edge all around as shown in Figure 3.

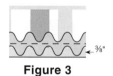

Figure 3

Step 4. Place the pillow backing piece right sides together with the handkerchief block; stitch all around, leaving a 6" opening on one side.

Step 5. Trim corner seams; turn right side out through opening. Press edges flat.

Step 6. Turn under opening edges ⅜"; press.

Step 7. Insert pillow form; hand-stitch opening closed to finish. ■

Dainty Handkerchief Pillow
Placement Diagram 12" x 12"

Small Floral Appliqué
10" x 10" Block
Make 2 for quilt
Make 1 for pillow

Large Floral Appliqué
18" x 28" Block
Make 1 for quilt

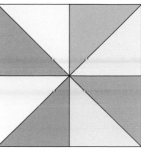

Pinwheel
10" x 10" Block
Make 18 for quilt
Make 3 for sham

A TOUCH OF ELEGANCE

Designs by Marinda Stewart

Pastel pink and green fabrics combine in piecing and appliqué in this elegant quilt, sham and pillow set.

PROJECT SPECIFICATIONS

Skill Level: Intermediate

Quilt Size: 88" x 89"

Pillow Sham Size: 36" x 26"

Pillow Size: 16" x 16" and 15" x 12½"

Block Size: 10" x 10" and 18" x 28"

Number of Blocks: 21, 3 and 1

SUPPLIES

- Batting 94" x 95" and two 34" x 24"
- Neutral color all-purpose thread
- Quilting thread
- Machine-embroidery threads to match fabrics
- 16" pillow form
- 16" x 12" pillow form
- 1½ yards fusible web
- 1⅜ yards fabric stabilizer
- Basic sewing tools and supplies

SPECIAL CUTTING INSTRUCTIONS

Step 1. Cut 57 total 4½" x 10½" L rectangles, 12 total 2½" x 4½" P rectangles and four total 2⅞" Q squares light yellow, light and dark green, and light and dark pink prints; cut each Q square in half on one diagonal to make eight Q triangles.

FABRIC Measurements based on 42" usable fabric width.	#STRIPS/PIECES	CUT
½ yard total light yellow prints		As per Special Cutting Instructions
1 yard white-with-green print	1	18½" x 28½" background rectangle
	3	10½" x 10½" background squares
1 yard rose-teal-green floral	6	5½" x 42" H/I
1½ yards muslin	2	34" x 24" sham linings
2 yards total light green prints	7	3" x 42"
	21	5⅞" squares
		Appliqué pieces as per pattern
2 yards total dark green prints	7	3" x 42"
	21	5⅞" squares
		Appliqué pieces as per pattern
2 yards total light pink prints	7	3" x 42"
	21	5⅞" squares
		Appliqué pieces as per pattern
2 yards total dark pink prints	7	4" x 42"
	21	5⅞" squares
		Appliqué pieces as per pattern
5¼ yards green stripe	2	1½" x 18½" A
	2	1½" x 30½" B
	1	1½" x 30½" C
	4	1½" x 42" D
	2	1½" x 10½" E
	5	2½" x 42" F/G
	6	1½" x 42" J/K
	4	3½" x 38" M
	4	3½" x 28" N
	4	21½" x 26½" sham backing
	2	10" x 13" patchwork pillow backing
	4	1½" x 14" O
	2	10½" x 16½" flower pillow backing
	9	2¼" x 42" binding
Backing	1	94" x 95"

QUILT

MAKING THE CENTER BLOCK

Step 1. Fold and crease the 18½" x 28½" background rectangle to mark the vertical and horizontal centers.

Step 2. Prepare templates for appliqué shapes using patterns given. *Note: The patterns have been reversed for fusible appliqué.*

Step 3. Trace shapes onto the paper side of the fusible web referring to patterns for number to cut. Cut out shapes, leaving a margin around each one.

Step 4. Fuse shapes to the wrong side of fabrics as directed on patterns for color, mixing light and dark prints referring to the photo of the quilt for suggestions. Cut out shapes on traced lines; remove paper backing. Select pieces needed for the center block; set aside all other pieces for corner blocks and pillow appliqué.

Step 5. Beginning with the large rose shape, lay pieces on the background rectangle in numerical order matching center of flower with crease lines. Insert stem pieces under rose design and fuse shapes in place; add bud shape and remaining leaf shapes referring to Figure 1.

Figure 1

Step 6. Cut an 18" x 28" rectangle fabric stabilizer; pin to the wrong side of the fused block.

Step 7. Using machine-embroidery thread to match fabric colors, machine satin-stitch around each shape to secure.

Step 8. When stitching is complete, remove fabric stabilizer; set aside center block.

COMPLETING THE PINWHEEL BLOCKS

Step 1. Cut each 5⅞" pink and green square in half on one diagonal to make a total of 168 triangles.

Step 2. To complete one Pinwheel block, refer to Figure 2 and sew a light pink print triangle to a dark green print triangle along the diagonal; repeat for two units. Sew a light green print triangle to a dark pink print triangle along the diagonal; repeat for two units. Press seams toward darker triangles.

Figure 2   **Figure 3**

Step 3. Join the units as shown in Figure 3 to complete one block; press seams in one direction. Repeat for 21 blocks; set aside four blocks for shams.

MAKING PATCHWORK FRAME

Step 1. Sew a 3" light pink print strip to a 3" dark green print strip with right sides together along length to make an X strip set; press seam toward darker fabric. Repeat for seven X strip sets. Repeat with dark pink print strips and light green print strips to make seven Y strip sets.

Step 2. Subcut X and Y strip sets into 3" segments as shown in Figure 4 on page 106; you will need 87 X and 88 Y segments. Set aside one X and two Y segments for Patchwork Pillow.

Figure 4

Figure 5

Step 3. Join one X segment with one Y segment to make a Four-Patch unit as shown in Figure 5; repeat for 86 units. Press seams in one direction. Set aside 32 Four-Patch units for shams and six for Patchwork Pillow.

MAKING SMALL FLORAL APPLIQUÉ BLOCKS

Step 1. Referring to Figure 6 for pieces needed and placement, arrange and fuse appliqué shapes in place in numerical order on each 10½" background square.

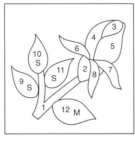
Figure 6

Step 2. Cut three 10" x 10" squares fabric stabilizer; pin a square to the wrong side of each fused square.

Step 3. Using machine-embroidery thread to match fabric colors, machine satin-stitch around each shape to secure.

Step 4. When stitching is complete, remove fabric stabilizer; set aside one block for pillow.

COMPLETING THE TOP

Step 1. Sew an A strip to the top and bottom, and B strips to opposite sides of the appliquéd center block; press seams toward strips.

Step 2. Join six Four-Patch units as shown in Figure 7; press seams in one direction. Repeat for eight six-unit strips.

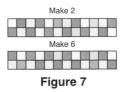
Make 2
Make 6
Figure 7

Step 3. Sew one Four-Patch strip to the B sides of the center unit referring to the Placement Diagram for positioning; press seams toward B.

Step 4. Join two Four-Patch strips along length referring to the Placement Diagram for positioning; press seam in one direction. Sew this strip to the bottom of the framed center block; press seams toward A.

Step 5. Join four Four-Patch strips along length referring to the Placement Diagram for positioning; press seams in one direction. Sew the pieced section to the top of the framed center block; press seams toward A.

Step 6. Sew C to the bottom of the pieced section; press seam toward C strip.

Step 7. Join three Pinwheel blocks referring to Figure 8; press seams in one direction. Sew the strip to the bottom of the pieced section; press seam toward C.

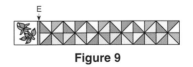
Figure 8

Step 8. Join the D strips on short ends to make one long strip; press seams open. Subcut strips into two 1½" x 71½" D strips. Sew the D strips to opposite long sides; press seams toward strips.

Step 9. Join six Pinwheel blocks to make a side row referring to Figure 9; repeat for two side rows.

E
Figure 9

Step 10. Add an E strip and a Small Floral Appliqué block to one end of each side row referring to the Placement Diagram for positioning. Sew a pieced strip to opposite long sides of the pieced center; press seams toward D strips.

Step 11. Join the F/G strips on short ends to make one long strip; press seams open. Subcut strip into one 2½" x 52½" F strip and two 2½" x 73½" G strips.

Step 12. Sew the F strip to the bottom and G strips to opposite long sides of the pieced center; press seams toward F and G strips.

Step 13. Join the H/I strips on short ends to make one long strip; press seams open. Subcut strip into one 5½" x 56½" H strip and two 5½" x 78½" I strips. Sew the H strip to the bottom and I strips to opposite long sides of the pieced center; press seams toward H and I.

Step 14. Join the J/K strips on short ends to make one long strip; press seams open. Subcut strip into one 1½" x 66½" J strip and two 1½" x 79½" K strips. Sew the J strip to the bottom and K strips to opposite long sides of the pieced center; press seams toward H and I.

Step 15. Join 20 L pieces along the 10½" sides in any color order to make an L side strip; repeat for two L side strips.

Step 16. Sew an L side strip to opposite long sides of the pieced center; press seam toward K. Trim excess L even with top edge of quilt top.

Step 17. Join 17 L pieces along the 10½" sides in any color order to make an L bottom strip. Sew a Pinwheel block to each end of the L bottom strip; press seams toward L.

Step 18. Sew the L bottom/block strip to the bottom of the pieced center to complete the pieced top.

Step 19. Sandwich batting between the completed top and prepared backing; pin and baste to hold layers together. Quilt as desired by hand or machine; remove pins or binding. Trim batting and backing even with quilt top.

Step 20. Join binding strips on short ends and cut

A Touch of Elegance Quilt
Placement Diagram 88" x 89"

to make four 92" lengths. Fold each strip in half with wrong sides together and press.

Step 21. Sew a binding strip to the top and bottom; trim ends even with quilt top edge as shown in Figure 10. Turn to the back side and hand-stitch in place. Sew the remaining two binding strips to opposite sides; trim ends ½" longer than quilt edge. Turn strip end in even with quilt edge and turn to back side as shown in Figure 11; hand-stitch in place.

Figure 10   **Figure 11**

PILLOW SHAM
COMPLETING THE SHAM

Step 1. Join two Pinwheel blocks referring to the Placement Diagram; press seams in one direction.

Step 2. Join four Four-Patch units to make a row; repeat for four rows. Press seams in one direction.

Step 3. Sew a Four-Patch row to opposite long sides

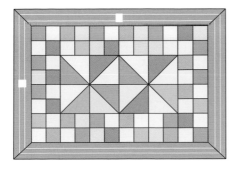

A Touch of Elegance Sham
Placement Diagram 36" x 26"

of the pieced block row; press seams away from block rows. Sew a Four-Patch row to remaining sides of the pieced section; press seams toward Four-Patch rows.

Step 4. Sandwich one 34" x 24" batting piece between one 34" x 24" muslin rectangle and the pieced top; pin or baste layers to hold. Repeat Steps 1–4 for second sham.

Step 5. Quilt and prepare binding and bind edges referring to the General Instructions.

Step 6. Center and sew an M strip to opposite long sides and an N strip to the remaining short sides of the pieced sections, mitering corners.

Step 7. Trim excess seam at miter to ¼"; press mitered seam open. Press remaining seam toward M and N strips to complete sham tops.

Step 8. Turn under one 26½" edge of each sham backing piece ¼" and press. Turn under the pressed edges ½" and stitch to hem.

Step 9. Overlap 5" and pin hemmed edges of two pieces right sides together with one quilted sham top; stitch all around. Turn right side out through overlapping backing to finish. Repeat for second sham.

PATCHWORK PILLOW
COMPLETING THE PILLOW

Step 1. Join three Four-Patch units to make a row referring to Figure 12; repeat for two rows. Press seams in one direction.

Make 1

Make 1

Figure 12

Y | X | Y

Figure 13

Step 2. Join the X and Y segments set aside in Step 2 for Making Patchwork Frame as shown in Figure 13; press seams in one direction. Sew the X-Y strip between the Four-Patch rows referring to the Placement Diagram for positioning to complete the pillow top.

Step 3. Turn under one 13" edge of each 10" x 13" backing piece ¼" and press. Turn under the pressed edges ½" and stitch to hem.

Step 4. Overlap 3" and pin hemmed edges of two pieces right sides together with the pieced pillow top; stitch all around. Turn right side out through overlapping backing to finish.

Step 5. Insert the 16" x 12" pillow form to finish.

APPLIQUÉ FLOWER PILLOW
COMPLETING THE FLOWER PILLOW

Step 1. Center and sew an O strip to each side of the remaining Small Floral Appliqué block, mitering corners. Trim excess seam at miter to ¼"; press mitered seam open. Press seams toward O.

Step 2. Join three P pieces on short ends to form a P strip as shown in Figure 14. Repeat for four strips; press seams in one direction.

P

Figure 14

Q
Q

Figure 15

Step 3. Sew a P strip to opposite sides of the framed block; press seams toward P.

Step 4. Join two different-fabric Q triangles to make a Q unit as shown in Figure 15; repeat for four Q units.

Step 5. Sew a Q unit to each end of the remaining P strips; press seams toward Q. Sew a P-Q strip to the remaining sides of the framed block; press seams toward O.

Step 6. Turn under one 16½" edge of each 10½" x 16½" backing piece ¼" and press. Turn under the pressed edges ½" and stitch to hem.

Step 7. Overlap 3" and pin hemmed edges of two pieces right sides together with the pieced pillow top; stitch all around. Turn right side out through overlapping backing to finish.

Step 8. Insert the 16" pillow form to finish. ▪

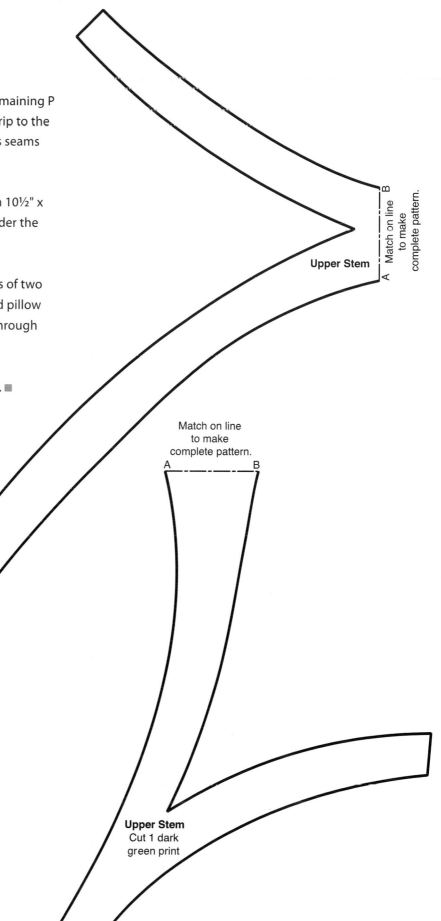

Appliqué Flower Pillow
Placement Diagram 16" x 16"

Upper Stem

A Match on line to make complete pattern. B

Match on line
to make
complete pattern.

A - - - - - B

Upper Stem
Cut 1 dark
green print

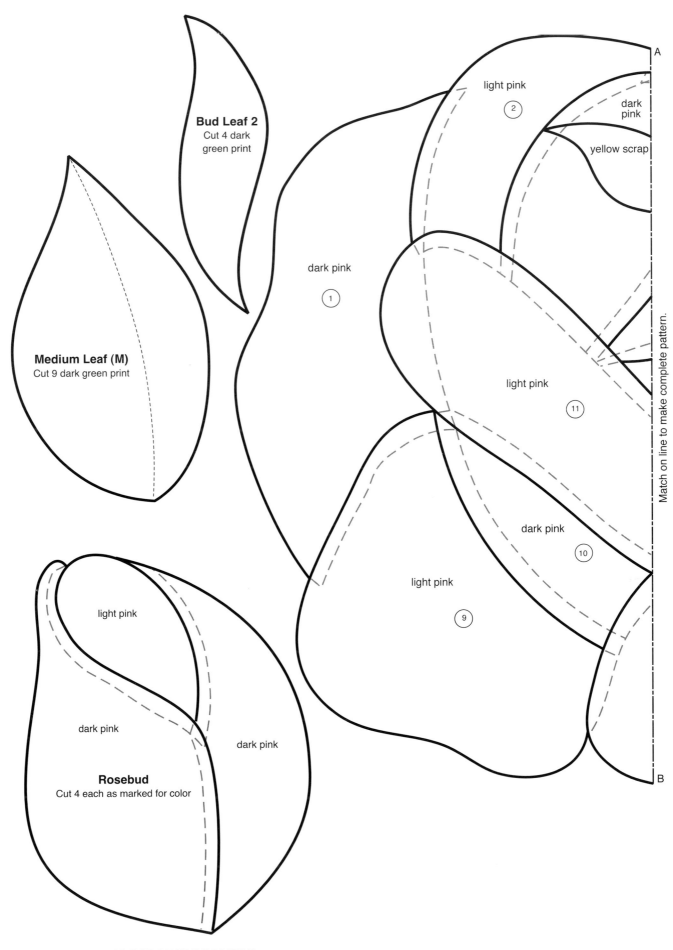

Bud Leaf 2
Cut 4 dark green print

light pink
②

dark pink

yellow scrap

Medium Leaf (M)
Cut 9 dark green print

dark pink
①

light pink
⑪

dark pink
⑩

light pink
⑨

light pink

dark pink

dark pink

Rosebud
Cut 4 each as marked for color

A

Match on line to make complete pattern.

B

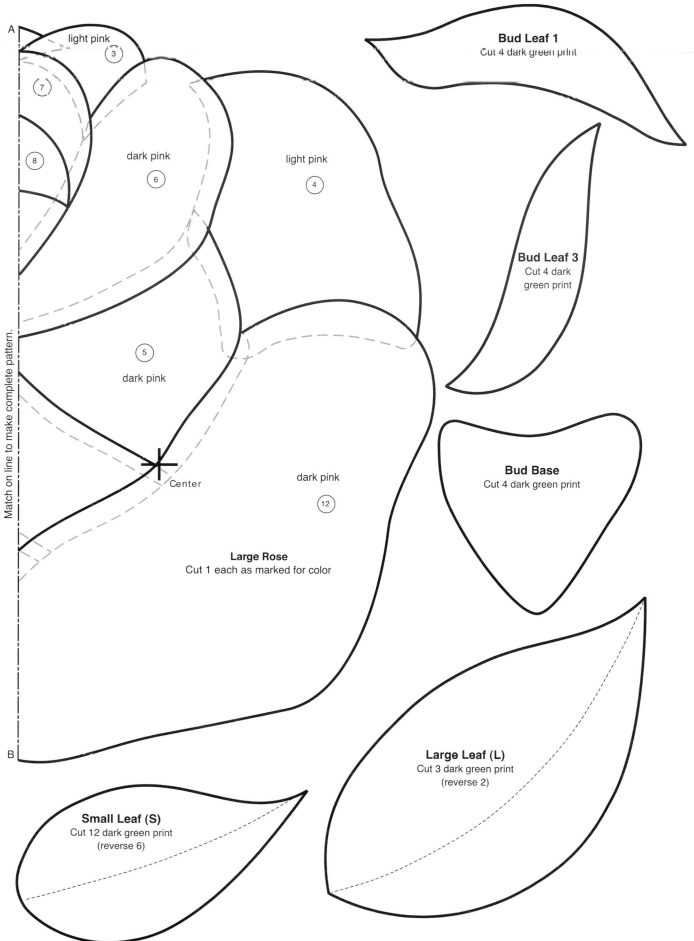

A

light pink
③

⑦

⑧

dark pink
⑥

light pink
④

Match on line to make complete pattern.

dark pink
⑤

Center

dark pink
⑫

Large Rose
Cut 1 each as marked for color

B

Bud Leaf 1
Cut 4 dark green print

Bud Leaf 3
Cut 4 dark
green print

Bud Base
Cut 4 dark green print

Large Leaf (L)
Cut 3 dark green print
(reverse 2)

Small Leaf (S)
Cut 12 dark green print
(reverse 6)

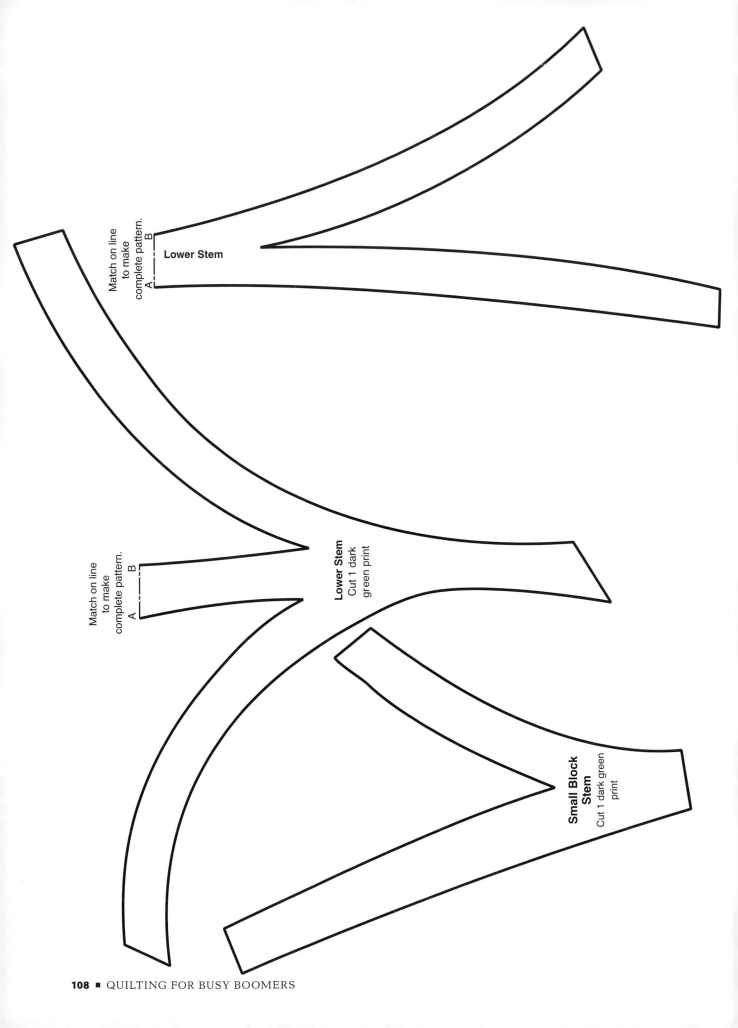

Match on line
to make
complete pattern.

B

A

Lower Stem

Match on line
to make
complete pattern.

B

A

Lower Stem
Cut 1 dark
green print

**Small Block
Stem**
Cut 1 dark green
print

PIECED QUILTS ARE STILL THE FAVORITE OF MANY

Pieced quilts are popular whether they are made with or without templates. If you prefer faster techniques, using a rotary cutter, ruler and mat make short work of cutting, and quick-piecing techniques using your sewing machine get the stitching job done in no time. Before you know it, your quilt top is ready for quilting.

SPECIAL PIECING TECHNIQUES

CREATING FOUR-PATCH BLOCKS WITH STRIP SETS

Four-Patch blocks or units can be pieced quickly by creating strip sets that are then subcut into segments. These segments are joined to create a block or unit. This same method works in many other types of multiple-strip units.

Step 1. To create a Four-Patch unit, join two same-width fabric strips with right sides together along the length to make a strip set; press seam toward the darkest fabric.

Step 2. Using a rotary ruler, mat and rotary cutter, subcut the strip set into 1½" (or other size as needed) segment.

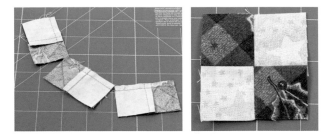

Step 3. Arrange two segments on a flat surface as shown.

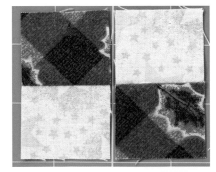

Step 4. Place the two segments right sides together, matching seams, and pin to hold.

Step 5. Chain-stitch multiple segments together and press to finish Four-Patch units.

MAKING FLYING GEESE UNITS

Step 1. Trace-and-stitch is a good, template-free technique for creating Flying Geese rectangle units. For each unit, two squares and one rectangle are needed to complete the three triangle shapes.

Step 2. Trace a diagonal line from corner to corner on the wrong side of the two squares. Place the first square at one end of the rectangle, with traced line slanting from one corner toward the center of the rectangle.

Step 3. Stitch on the traced line, press and trim. ***Note:*** *Start the stitching at the center of the rectangle instead of at the corner for easier initial needle insertion.*

Step 4. Position the second square on the opposite end of the rectangle, with traced seam slanting opposite and crossing previous seam.

Step 5. Stitch on the traced line, press and trim.

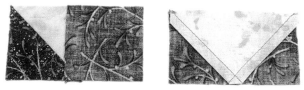

Step 6. Completed right side and wrong side of Flying Geese unit.

English paper piecing is a technique that uses paper shapes as the foundations to accurately prepare the patchwork pieces. The trimmed paper shape is basted, pinned or glued to the back side center of a fabric patch that has seam allowances added. The seam allowances are folded over the paper edge and basted into the finished size. The prepared shapes are then joined using a whipstitch along the folded edges of the fabrics.

While many shapes may be used with this technique, including triangles, trapezoids, squares and diamonds, the most familiar shape is the hexagon seen in traditional Grandmother's Flower Garden settings. Work in progress is portable, space conserving, comfortably repetitive and simple.

Preparing Patches

Step 1. Make photocopies of the design on regular-weight white paper. ***Note:*** *There are many commercial shapes that can be purchased.*

Step 2. Carefully cut out each hexagon shape.

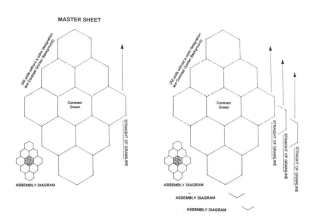

Step 3. Prepare a cutting template by adding a ¼"

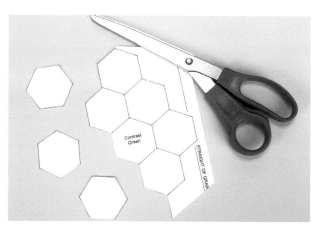

seam allowance to one paper hexagon. Trace and cut out fabric patches using this template.

Step 4. Center and secure one paper shape against the wrong side of the fabric patch. **Note:** *Use fabric glue stick, straight pin or quick basting stitches to hold the paper shape in place.*

Step 5. Fold and finger-press or pinch the first fabric edge back precisely at the paper edge. Using a single thread baste through fabric and paper layers, stopping near opposite edge and corner of enclosed paper shape.

Step 6. Fold and finger-press the second edge back at the paper edges as before, this time including the folded-over seam allowance from the first side. **Note:** *Work with the front side of patch toward the stitcher. This will allow the knot to remain visible for easier clipping and basting removal after patchwork is complete.*

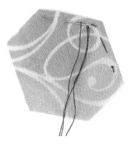

Step 7. Continue to fold and finger-press each succeeding edge as before for all remaining edges. Secure basting end with a small backstitch with needle piercing only the top fabric layer, easily visible from front for removal later. Trim thread, leaving a ¼" tail.

Step 8. Prepare all the hexagon shapes required for specified construction unit. Position in layout order for reference during joining.

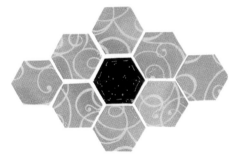

Joining Patches

Step 1. Begin with center and one adjacent hexagon. Identify the edges to be joined, and then layer them right sides together.

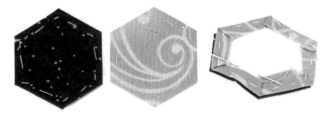

Step 2. Single-thread a needle with matching thread, with a knot at one end. At top corner, insert needle under seam allowance and out corner tip of top patch.

Step 3. Insert needle through lower layer and upper layer fabric folds exactly at the corner. Needle should catch only one or two threads at the folded edge of the patch and miss or only barely pierce enclosed paper edge. Secure this corner—and each corner throughout construction—by taking a second stitch exactly through the corner.

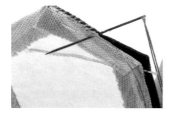

Step 4. Using fairly close stitches (12–14 per inch), continue whipstitching along the edges to be joined.

Step 5. At the opposite corner, secure with two stitches exactly through corner. (Contrast thread is used here to show the stitch-length gauge.)

Step 6. To tie off or end a sequence (or when thread in needle has been used up), slip needle through the final stitch loop before it is pulled tight to anchor. Insert needle under top layer of seam allowance, to exit toward the patch's center. Pull thread up and cut the tail even with the seam allowance edge. If adding another patch, skip step 6 and repeat steps 1–5 for next patch.

Step 7. Open patches flat.

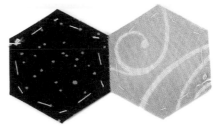

Step 8. Position and identify the next edges to be joined; layer the hexagon patch right sides together. Insert needle between fabric layers within fold tunnel and exit the needle at the halfway point. Pass the needle through both patches at the center point, and then repeat a stitch in place to tack the edges. ***Note:*** *When joining the six hexagons around a center, always work from the outer edge back toward the center so that the needle will end at the best corner for continuing on.*

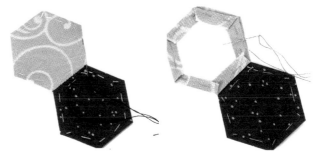

Step 9. Pass the needle through the tunnel in the fold to the top corner. Complete corner stitches; then stitch down along the edges to the opposite corner and repeat the anchor stitches.

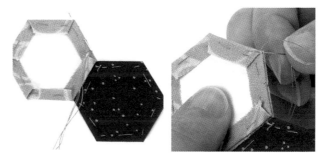

Step 10. Pivot the second edge of the upper patch to align to its appropriate mate. Secure corner, whipstitch across edge and secure at opposite corner. ***Note:*** *It may be necessary to fold the work whenever the edge connection process requires the*

pivot. Don't let the stiffness of the paper interfere with stitching accurately.

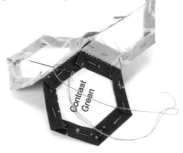

Step 11. Open the seam; then position and repeat the joining process for each subsequent hexagon to complete the ring around the center. When the unit is complete, press lightly with a moderately warm iron.

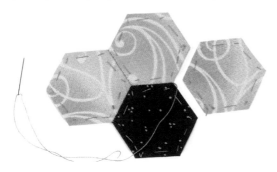

Removing Paper

Step 1. To remove basting, work from the front side to first snip off basting knots, and then slip final anchoring stitch free; finally, pull basting from each patch.

Step 2. Turn patchwork to the back side, and slip fingers or tweezers under overlapping seam allowance to lift paper edge; remove each paper shape.

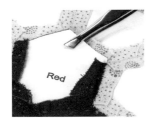

PAPER PIECING INSTRUCTIONS

Paper piecing is used to make very accurate blocks, provides stability for weak fabrics, and adds body and weight to the finished quilt.

Piecing on paper results in complete accuracy. Quilters usually use this method when piecing with very small pieces or when stitching a complicated pieced unit or block.

The patterns provided for paper piecing have been reversed. Because you stitch on the marked side of the paper, but the opposite side is the finished fabric right side, the pattern must be reversed.

Step 1. Begin by making the copies as directed. Measure the finished paper foundations to insure accuracy in copying.

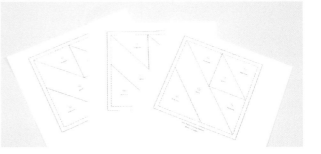

Step 2. To paper-piece, place a scrap of fabric larger than the lined space on the unmarked side of the paper in the No. 1 position.

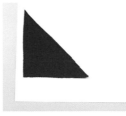

Step 3. Place piece 2 right sides together with piece 1.

Step 4. Pin on seam line and fold back to check that the piece will cover space 2 before stitching.

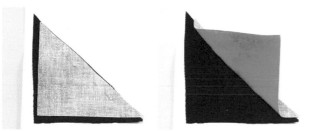

Step 5. Use a smaller stitch than for normal sewing—12–14 stitches per inch or 2mm to allow for ease in removing foundation later. Stitch along line on the lined side of the paper—fabric will not be visible. Sew several stitches beyond the beginning and end of the line. Backstitching is not required, because another fabric seam will cover this seam.

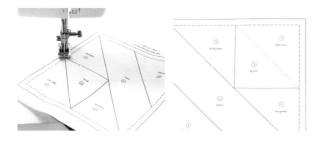

Step 6. Trim seam to ⅛".

Step 7. Remove pin; finger-press piece 2 flat.

Step 8. Continue adding pieces in numerical order in the same manner until all pieces are stitched to paper.

Step 9. Trim excess to outside line (¼" larger all around than finished size of the block).

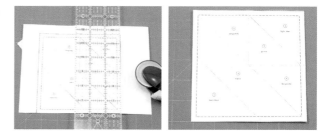

Step 10. Paper is removed when blocks are complete and stitched together, or as directed in the patterns.

SPRINGTIME TABLE MAT

Design by Connie Kauffman

The colors of springtime shine in this simple-to-stitch table mat.

PROJECT SPECIFICATIONS

Skill Level: Beginner

Table Mat Size: 24" x 24"

SUPPLIES

- Batting 25" x 25"
- All-purpose thread to match fabrics
- Quilting thread
- Basic sewing tools and supplies

COMPLETING THE TOP

Step 1. Mark a diagonal line from corner to corner on the wrong side of each C and H square.

Step 2. Referring to Figure 1, place a C square right sides together on opposite ends of B; stitch on the marked lines.

Figure 1

Figure 2

Step 3. Trim seams to ¼" and press C to the right side referring to Figure 2.

Step 4. Repeat Steps 2 and 3 on the remaining corners of B to complete one B-C unit referring to Figure 3; repeat to make four B-C units.

FABRIC Measurements based on 42" usable fabric width.	#STRIPS/PIECES	CUT	#PIECES	SUBCUT
☐ ¼ yard white tonal	2	2" x 42"	32	2" C squares
■ ⅓ yard dark blue tonal	1	3½" x 42"	8	5" F rectangles
	1	3½" x 42"	4	6½" B rectangles
			4	3½" E squares
☐ ⅓ yard yellow tonal	1	2" x 42"	16	2" H squares
	1	6½" A square		
▨ ⅝ yard yellow/blue floral	1	6½" x 42"	4	6½" D squares
	1	3½" x 42"	8	2" G rectangles
	1	9¾" square		Cut on both diagonals to make 4 I triangles
☐ Backing		25" x 25"		

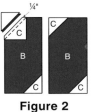

Figure 3

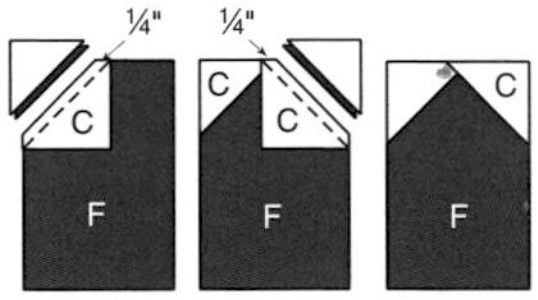

Figure 4

Step 5. Referring to Figure 4, sew C to one corner of F; trim seam to ¼" and press C to the right side. Repeat with a second C on the same end of F to complete one C-F unit, again referring to Figure 4. Repeat to complete eight C-F units.

Step 6. Repeat Step 5 with G and H to complete eight G-H units referring to Figure 5.

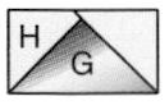

Figure 5

Step 7. Sew a B-C unit to opposite sides of A as shown in Figure 6; press seams toward A.

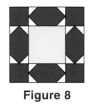

Figure 6

Figure 7

Step 8. Sew an E square to opposite ends of each of the remaining two B-C units as shown in Figure 7; press seams toward E.

Step 9. Sew a B-C-E unit to the remaining sides of A to complete the center unit as shown in Figure 8; press seams away from A.

Figure 8

Figure 9

Step 10. Sew a G-H unit to the F end of a C-F unit as shown in Figure 9; press seam toward C-F. Repeat to make eight C-F-G-H units.

Step 11. Sew a C-F-G-H unit to opposite sides of D to make a side unit as shown in Figure 10; press seams toward D. Repeat to make four side units.

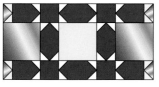

Figure 10

Figure 11

Step 12. Sew a side unit to opposite sides of the center unit to complete the center row as shown in Figure 11; press seams toward the side units.

Step 13. Sew I to each end of each remaining side unit to make the top row referring to Figure 12; press seams toward I. Repeat to make the bottom row.

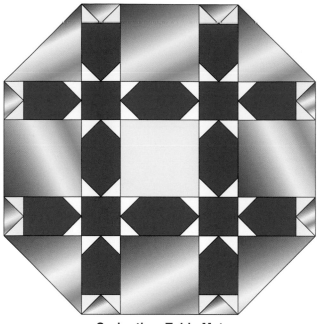

Springtime Table Mat
Placement Diagram 24" x 24"

Figure 12

Step 14. Sew the top and bottom rows to the center row to complete the pieced top; press seams away from the center row.

COMPLETING THE QUILT

Step 1. Lay the batting square on a flat surface with the backing square right side up on top; place the pieced top right sides together with the backing square and pin layers to hold.

Step 2. Trim excess batting and backing edges even with the pieced top; stitch all around, leaving a 5" opening on one side.

Step 3. Turn right side out through the opening and press flat.

Step 4. Turn opening seams to the inside; press and hand-stitch closed.

Step 5. Hand- or machine-quilt as desired to finish. ∎

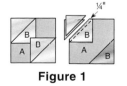
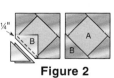

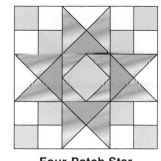

Four-Patch Star
12" x 12" Block
Make 1

TABLE GRACE

Design by Julie Weaver

A star block graces the center of this versatile table mat, which is the ideal centerpiece for any table.

PROJECT SPECIFICATIONS

Skill Level: Beginner
Quilt Size: 24" x 24"
Block Size: 12" x 12"
Number of Blocks: 1

SUPPLIES

- Batting 30" x 30"
- All-purpose thread to match fabrics
- Quilting thread
- Basic sewing tools and supplies

COMPLETING THE BLOCKS

Step 1. Draw a diagonal line from corner to corner on the wrong side of each B square.

Step 2. Referring to Figure 1, place a B square on opposite corners of A and stitch on the marked lines; trim seam allowances to ¼" and press B to the right side.

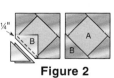

Figure 1   **Figure 2**

Step 3. Repeat Step 2 on the two remaining corners of A to complete the A-B center unit as shown in Figure 2.

FABRIC Measurements based on 42" usable fabric width.	#STRIPS/PIECES	CUT	#PIECES	SUBCUT
¼ yard cream tonal	1	5¼" x 42"	1	5¼" E square
			8	2½" F squares
¼ yard blue tonal	1	5¼" x 42"	1	5¼" C square
			2	1½" x 12½" H
			2	1½" x 14½" I
½ yard blue floral	1	5¼" x 42"	2	5¼" D squares
			4	2½" B squares
	2	4" x 42"	2	15½" L rectangles
			2	22½" M rectangles
⅔ yard light green tonal	1	4½" x 42"	1	4½" A square
			8	2½" G squares
	2	1" x 42"	2	14½" J rectangles
			2	15½" K rectangles
	2	1½" x 22½" N		
	2	1½" x 24½" O		
	3	2½" x 42" binding		
Backing		30" x 30"		

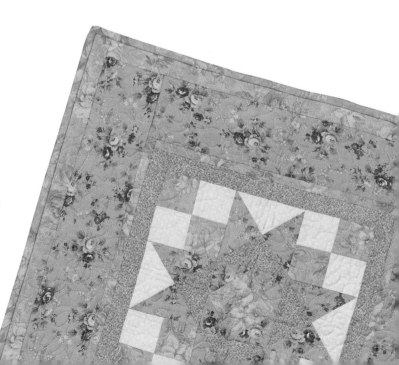

Step 4. Cut each C, D and E square on both diagonals to make four each C and E triangles and eight D triangles.

Step 5. Sew C to D and D to E as shown in Figure 3; press seams toward D. Repeat to make four each C-D and D-E units.

Figure 3

Step 6. Sew a C-D unit to a D-E unit to complete a side unit as shown in Figure 4; press seam toward the C-D unit. Repeat to make four side units.

Figure 4

Step 7. Sew F to G; press seam toward G. Repeat to make eight F-G units.

Step 8. Join two F-G units as shown in Figure 5 to complete a corner unit; press seam in one direction. Repeat to make four corner units.

Figure 5

Step 9. Sew a side unit to opposite sides of the A-B center unit to complete the center row as shown in Figure 6; press seams toward the side units.

Figure 7

Step 10. Sew an F-G corner unit to opposite sides of each remaining side unit to make the top and bottom rows referring to Figure 7; press seams toward the side units.

Figure 7

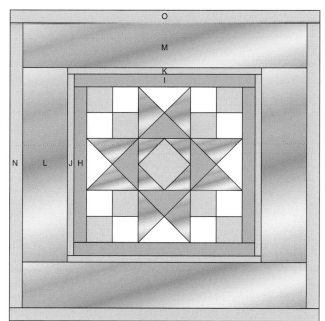

Table Grace
Placement Diagram 24" x 24"

Step 11. Join the rows referring to the block drawing to complete the Four-Patch Star block; press seams in one direction.

COMPLETING THE QUILT

Step 1. Sew an H strip to opposite sides and I strips to the top and bottom of the pieced block; press seams toward H and I strips.

Step 2. Repeat Step 1 with J–O strips referring to the Placement Diagram and pressing seams toward newly added strips as they are added to complete the pieced top.

Step 3. Layer, quilt, prepare binding and bind edges referring to the Finishing Instructions. ■

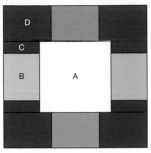

Fourth of July
12" x 12" Block
Make 13

FOURTH OF JULY PICNIC BLANKET

Design by Holly Daniels

Select a variety of red and blue prints to make this quilt for your holiday picnic.

PROJECT SPECIFICATIONS

Skill Level: Beginner

Quilt Size: 61" x 61"

Block Size: 12" x 12"

Number of Blocks: 13

SUPPLIES

- Batting 67" x 67"
- All-purpose thread to match fabrics
- Quilting thread
- Basic sewing tools and supplies

COMPLETING THE BLOCKS

Step 1. Sort C pieces into 13 sets of four same-fabric pieces; repeat with D pieces.

Step 2. To complete one block, select one set each of C and D pieces, four B pieces and one A square.

Step 3. Sew C to the 3½" ends of two B rectangles as shown in Figure 1; press seams toward B.

Figure 1

Figure 2

Step 4. Sew the B-C units to opposite sides of A as shown in Figure 2; press seams away from A.

FABRIC Measurements based on 42" usable fabric width.		#STRIPS/ PIECES	CUT	#PIECES	SUBCUT
	7 fat quarters blue reproduction prints	13	3½" x 21"	52	4½" B rectangles
	7 fat quarters red reproduction prints	2	3½" x 21" D each 6 fabrics	4	4½" D rectangles each strip
		2	1½" x 21" C each 6 fabrics	4	3½" C rectangles each strip
		1	3½" x 21" D	4	4½" D rectangles
		1	1½" x 21" C	4	3½" C rectangles
		1	9¾" square each 2 fabrics; cut on both diagonals to make 8 F triangles		
		1	5⅛" square each 2 fabrics; cut in half on 1 diagonal to make 4 G triangles		
	1½ yards white solid	3	6½" x 42"	13	6½" A squares
		8	3½" x 42"	20	14" E strips
	1⅝ yards red-white-and-blue print	6	5½" x 42" H/I		
		7	2¼" x 42" binding		
	Backing		67" x 67"		

Step 5. Sew B between two D rectangles to make a B-D unit as shown in Figure 3; press seams toward D. Repeat to make two B-D units.

Figure 3

Step 6. Sew a B-D unit to opposite sides of the A-B-C unit to complete one Fourth of July block referring to Figure 4; press seams toward the B-D units. Repeat to make 13 blocks.

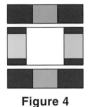

Figure 4

COMPLETING THE QUILT

Step 1. Sew one E strip to one short side of F matching one square end of E on one square side of F as shown in Figure 5; press seam toward F.

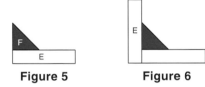

Figure 5   **Figure 6**

Step 2. Repeat with a second E strip on the remaining square side of F as shown in Figure 6; press seam toward F.

Step 3. Using a rotary cutter and straightedge, trim E even with the long edge of F to complete an E-F unit as shown in Figure 7; repeat to make eight E-F units.

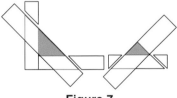

Figure 7

Step 4. Center and sew an E strip to the long side of a G triangle; press seam toward G.

Step 5. Using a rotary cutter and straightedge, trim E even with the short edges of G to complete an E-G unit, again referring to Figure 7; repeat to make four E-G units.

Step 6. Arrange and join the blocks with the E-F and E-G units in diagonal rows referring to Figure 8; press seams in adjacent rows in opposite directions.

Fourth of July Picnic Blanket
Placement Diagram 61" x 61"

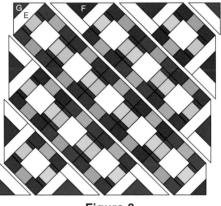

Figure 8

Step 7. Join the rows to complete the pieced top; press seams from the center row toward the side rows.

Step 8. Join the H/I strips on the short ends with right sides together to make one long strip; press seams open. Subcut strip into two 51½" H strips and two 61½" I strips.

Step 9. Sew H strips to opposite sides and I strips to the remaining sides of the pieced center; press seams toward H and I strips to complete the pieced top.

Step 10. Layer quilt, prepare binding and bind edges referring to the Finishing Instructions. ■

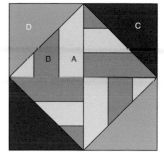

Sunflower
17¼" x 17¼" Block
Make 9

FIELD OF
SUNFLOWERS

Design by Connie Rand

I've never had much success growing sunflowers in
my garden. This sunflower quilt was much easier!

PROJECT SPECIFICATIONS

Skill Level: Beginner

Quilt Size: 57¾" x 57¾"

Block Size: 17¼" x 17¼"

Number of Blocks: 9

SUPPLIES

- Batting 64" x 64"
- All-purpose thread to match fabrics
- Quilting thread
- Basic sewing tools and supplies

FABRIC Measurements based on 42" usable fabric width.	#STRIPS/ PIECES	CUT	#PIECES	SUBCUT
1 yard light purple batik	9	3½" x 42" A		
1 yard blue stars batik	3	9½" x 42"	9	9½" squares; cut on 1 diagonal to make 18 D triangles
1⅜ yards medium purple batik	6	2¼" x 42" binding		
	9	3½" x 42" B		
1½ yards sunflower batik	6	3½" x 42" E/F		
	3	9½" x 42"	9	9½" squares; cut on 1 diagonal to make 18 C triangles
Backing		64" x 64"		

COMPLETING THE BLOCKS

Step 1. Sew a B strip between two A strips with right sides together along the length; press seams toward B. Repeat to make three A-B-A strip sets.

Step 2. Subcut the A-B-A strip sets into nine 9½" square segments; cut each square on one diagonal to make 18 A-B-A units as shown in Figure 1.

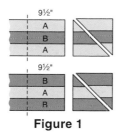

Figure 1

Step 3. Repeat Steps 1 and 2 to make 18 B-A-B units, again referring to Figure 1.

Step 4. To complete one Sunflower block, sew an A-B-A unit to D, referring to Figure 2, to complete one A-B-A-D unit; press seam toward D. Repeat to make two units.

Figure 2

Step 5. Repeat Step 4 with C and B-A-B to make two B-A-B-C units, again referring to Figure 2.

Step 6. Join one each A-B-A-D and B-A-B-C unit to make a row, again referring to Figure 2; press seam toward the B-A-B-C unit. Repeat to make two rows.

Step 7. Join the rows referring to the block drawing to complete one Sunflower block; press seam in one direction. Repeat to make nine blocks.

COMPLETING THE QUILT

Step 1. Join three blocks to make a row as shown in

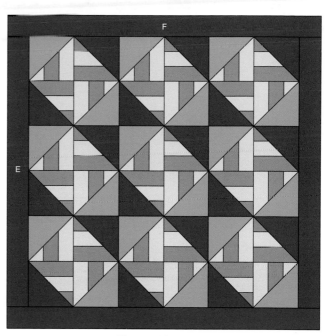

Field of Sunflowers
Placement Diagram
57¾" x 57¾"

Figure 3; press seams in one direction. Repeat to make three rows.

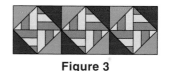

Figure 3

Step 2. Join the rows to complete the pieced center; press seams in one direction.

Step 3. Join E/F strips with right sides together on short ends to make one long strip; press seams open. Subcut strips into two each 52¼" E and 58¼" F strips.

Step 4. Sew E strips to opposite sides and F strips to the top and bottom of the pieced center to complete the quilt top; press seams toward E and F strips.

Step 5. Layer, quilt, prepare binding and bind edges referring to the Finishing Instructions. ■

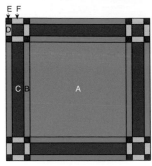

Picture This
12" x 12" Block
Make 12

PICTURE THIS

Design by Julie Weaver

A truck novelty print is featured in the center of this quick-to-stitch quilt.

PROJECT SPECIFICATIONS

Skill Level: Beginner

Quilt Size: 49" x 62"

Block Size: 12" x 12"

Number of Blocks: 12

SUPPLIES

- Batting 55" x 68"
- All-purpose thread to match fabrics
- Quilting thread
- Basic sewing tools and supplies

COMPLETING THE BLOCKS

Step 1. To complete one Picture This block, sew a C strip between two B strips to make a B-C strip set; press seams toward B. Repeat to make 12 B-C strip sets.

Step 2. Subcut the B-C strip sets into (48) 8½" B-C units as shown in Figure 1.

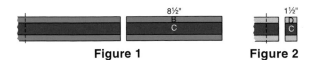

| Figure 1 | Figure 2 |

Step 3. Sew a C strip between two D strips to make a C-D strip set; press seams toward C. Repeat to make two C-D strip sets.

Step 4. Subcut the C-D strip sets into (48) 1½" C-D units as shown in Figure 2.

FABRIC — Measurements based on 42" usable fabric width.	#STRIPS/ PIECES	CUT	#PIECES	SUBCUT
½ yard yellow mottled	4	1" x 42" D		
	3	1½" x 42" F		
	1	1½" x 42"	6	1½" G squares
¾ yard red dot	6	1" x 42" E		
	3	1½" x 42" I		
	2	1½" x 40½" J		
	1	4" x 42"	4	4" P squares
			4	1½" M squares
	1	8½" x 42"	17	1½" H strips
⅞ yard truck print	3	8½" x 42"	12	8½" A squares
1¼ yards blue dot	14	1½" x 42" C		
	5	4" x 42" N/O		
1¾ yards green print	24	1" x 42" B		
	3	1½" x 42" K		
	2	1½" x 40½" L		
	6	2¼" x 42" binding		
Backing		55" x 68"		

Step 5. Sew an F strip between two E strips to make an E-F strip set; press seams toward E. Repeat to make three strip sets.

Step 6. Subcut the E-F strip sets into (96) E-F units as shown in Figure 3.

| Figure 3 | Figure 4 |

Step 7. To complete one block, sew a B-C unit to opposite sides of A as shown in Figure 4; press seams toward A.

Step 8. Sew an E-F unit to opposite sides of a C-D unit as shown in Figure 5 to complete a corner unit; press seams toward the C-D unit. Repeat to make four corner units.

Figure 5

Step 9. Sew a corner unit to each end of two B-C units to make two side strips as shown in Figure 6; press seams toward the corner units.

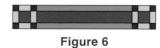

Figure 6

Step 10. Sew the side strips to the remaining sides of A to complete one Picture This block; press seams toward side strips. Repeat to make 12 blocks.

COMPLETING THE QUILT

Step 1. Join three Picture This blocks with two H strips to make a block row as shown in Figure 7; press seams toward H. Repeat to make four block rows.

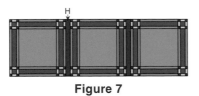

Figure 7

Step 2. Join three H strips and two G squares to make a sashing row referring to Figure 8; press seams toward H. Repeat to make three sashing rows.

Figure 8

Step 3. Join the block rows with the sashing rows to complete the pieced center; press seams toward the sashing rows.

Step 4. Join the I strips on short ends to make one long strip; press seams open. Subcut strip into two 51½" I strips.

Step 5. Sew an I strip to opposite long sides and J strips to the top and bottom of the pieced center; press seams toward I and J strips.

Step 6. Join the K strips on short ends to make one long strip; press seams open. Subcut strip into two 53½" K strips.

Step 7. Sew K strips to opposite long sides of the pieced center; press seams toward K strips.

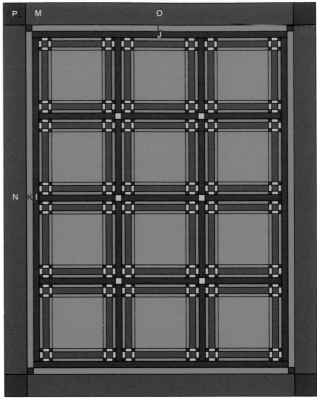

Picture This
Placement Diagram 49" x 62"

Step 8. Sew an M square to each end of each L strip; press seams toward L. Sew an M-L strip to the top and bottom of the pieced center; press seams toward the M-L strips.

Step 9. Join the N/O strips on short ends to make one long strip; press seams open. Subcut strip into two 55½" N and two 42½" O strips.

Step 10. Sew N strips to opposite long sides of the pieced center; press seams toward N strips.

Step 11. Sew a P square to each end of each O strip; press seams toward O. Sew an O-P strip to the top and bottom of the pieced center to complete the pieced top; press seams toward the O-P strips

Step 12. Layer, quilt, prepare binding and bind edges referring to the Finishing Instructions. ∎

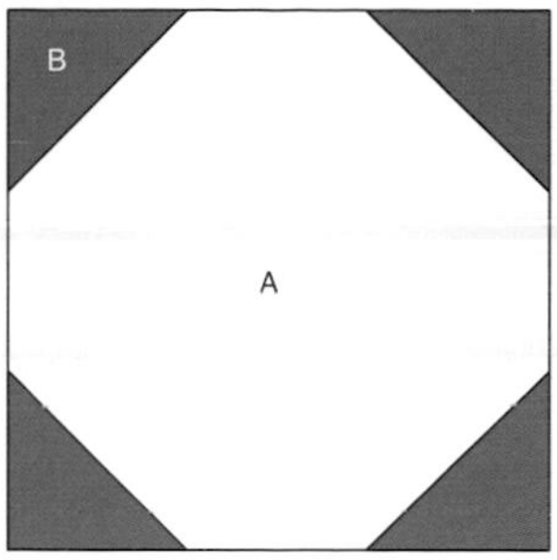

Snowball
9" x 9" Block
Make 24

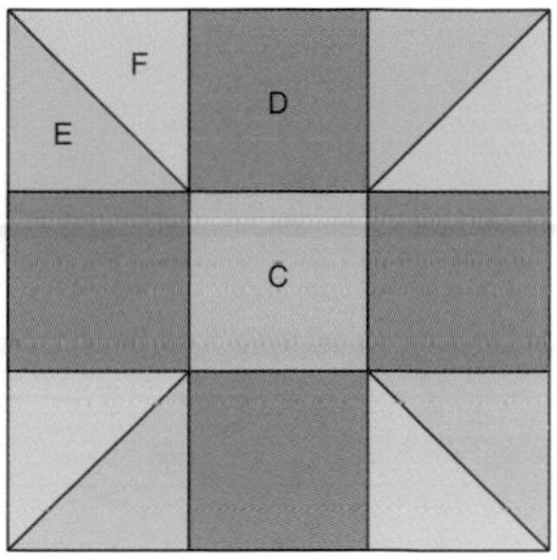

Puzzle
9" x 9" Block
Make 15

HAPPY DAYS

Design by Rochelle Martin

Baby boomers all remember the show *Happy Days* staring Henry Winkler and Ron Howard. This quilt celebrates those happy days.

PROJECT SPECIFICATIONS

Skill Level: Beginner

Quilt Size: 73" x 98½"

Block Size: 9" x 9"

Number of Blocks: 39

SUPPLIES

- Batting 79" x 105"
- All-purpose thread to match fabrics
- Quilting thread
- Basic sewing tools and supplies

COMPLETING THE PUZZLE BLOCKS

Step 1. Draw a diagonal line from corner to corner on the wrong side of each E square.

Step 2. Place one E square right sides together with one F square and stitch ¼" on each side of the marked line as shown in Figure 1; cut apart on the marked line to make two E-F units, again referring to Figure 1. Repeat with all E and F squares to complete 60 E-F units.

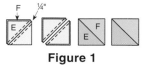

Figure 1

Step 3. To complete one Puzzle block, sew C between two D squares to make the center row; press seams toward D.

FABRIC Measurements based on 42" usable fabric width.	#STRIPS/PIECES	CUT	#PIECES	SUBCUT
⅔ yard lime print	3	3⅞" x 42"	30	3⅞" F squares
	2	7¼" squares; cut on 1 diagonal to make 4 H triangles		
1⅛ yards blue/green print	3	3⅞" x 42"	30	3⅞" E squares
	2	3½" x 42"	15	3½" C squares
	2	14" squares; cut on both diagonals to make 8 blue/green G triangles		
1⅛ yards royal blue/green print	8	3½" x 42"	96	3½" B squares
	7	4½" x 42" I/J		
2⅛ yards pink print	5	3½" x 42"	60	3½" D squares
	8	4½" x 42" M/N		
	2	14" squares; cut on both diagonals to make 8 pink G triangles		
3¼ yards white print	6	9½" x 42"	24	9½" A squares
	8	3½" x 42" K/L		
	9	2¼" x 42" binding		
Backing		79" x 105"		

Step 4. Sew D between two E-F units to make the top row as shown in Figure 2; press seams toward D. Repeat to make the bottom row.

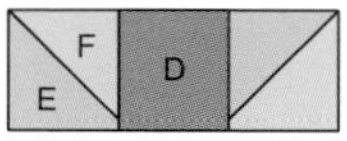

Figure 2

Step 5. Sew the center row between the top and bottom rows to complete one Puzzle block referring to the block drawing; press seams toward the center row. Repeat to make 15 blocks.

COMPLETING THE SNOWBALL BLOCKS

Step 1. Mark a diagonal line from corner to corner on the wrong side of each B square.

Step 2. Referring to Figure 3, place a B square right sides together on each corner of A and stitch on the marked line; trim seams to ¼" and press B to the right side to complete one Snowball block. Repeat to make 24 blocks.

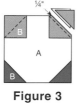

Figure 3

COMPLETING THE QUILT

Step 1. Arrange and join the pieced blocks in diagonal rows with the H and G triangles, alternating the blocks in each row as shown in Figure 4; press seams in adjacent rows in opposite directions.

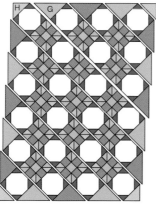

Figure 4

Step 2. Join the rows to complete the pieced center; press seams in one direction.

Step 3. Join the I/J strips with right sides together on short ends to make one long strip; press seams open. Subcut strip into two 77" I strips and two 59½" J strips.

Step 4. Repeat Step 3 with K/L strips; subcut strip into two 85" K strips and two 65½" L strips.

Step 5. Repeat Step 3 with M/N strips; subcut strip into two 91" M strips and two 73½" N strips.

Step 6. Sew the I strips to opposite long sides and J strips to the top and bottom of the pieced center; press seams toward I and J strips.

Step 7. Repeat Step 6 with K and L strips, and M and N strips to complete the pieced top; press seams toward newly added strip after each addition.

Step 8. Layer, quilt, prepare binding and bind edges referring to the Finishing Instructions. ■

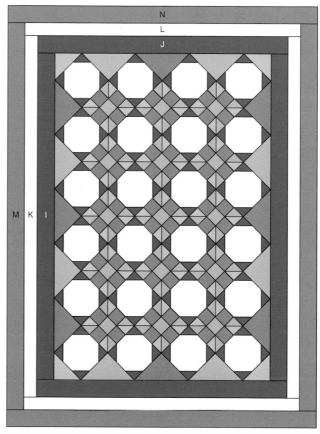

Happy Days
Placement Diagram 73" x 98½"

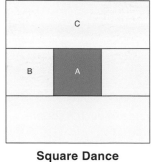

Square Dance
6" x 6" Block
Make 84

SQUARE DANCE

Design by Jill Reber

Reminiscent of our grandmothers' times, this scrappy reproduction quilt has a very soft touch.

PROJECT NOTES

You may prefer to cut individual pieces for each block rather than using strip-pieced units. The advantage of cutting individual pieces is that it creates more variety in the blocks. Instead of one solid color being combined with the same print in multiple blocks, you can vary the combinations.

Using strip-pieced units speeds up the process by eliminating the need to cut one piece at a time and stitch those pieces together for the B-A-B center units.

PROJECT SPECIFICATIONS

Skill Level: Beginner

Quilt Size: 64" x 76"

Block Size: 6" x 6"

Number of Blocks: 84

SUPPLIES

- Batting 70" x 82"
- All-purpose thread to match fabrics
- Quilting thread
- Basic sewing tools and supplies

COMPLETING THE SQUARE DANCE BLOCKS

Step 1. Select one A strip, two matching B strips and eight matching C rectangles.

FABRIC Measurements based on 42" usable fabric width.	#STRIPS/ PIECES	CUT	#PIECES	SUBCUT
7 fat quarters pastel solids	3	2½" x 21" A each fabric		
⅓ yard each 21 pastel prints	2	2½" x 21" B each fabric		
	1	6½" x 42" each fabric	8	2½" C rectangles each fabric
			6	2½" F rectangles each fabric; set aside 10 F for another project
1⅛ yards cream solid	6	2½" x 42" D/E		
	7	2¼" x 42" binding		
Backing		70" x 82"		

Step 2. Sew the A strip between two B strips with right sides together along the length; press seams toward the B strip.

Step 3. Subcut the B-A-B strip set into four 2½" B-A-B units as shown in Figure 1.

Figure 1   **Figure 2**

Step 4. Sew a matching C rectangle to each side of one B-A-B unit as shown in Figure 2 to complete one Square Dance block; repeat to make four matching blocks.

Step 5. Repeat with the remaining A and B strips, and C rectangles to complete 84 Square Dance blocks.

COMPLETING THE QUILT

Step 1. Select eight Square Dance blocks and join to make a row referring to Figure 3; press seams toward upright blocks, again referring to Figure 3. Repeat to make 10 rows.

Figure 3

Step 2. Join the rows, alternating placement of blocks referring to the Placement Diagram; press seams in one direction.

Step 3. Join the D-E strips right sides together on the short ends to make one long strip; press seams open. Subcut the strip into two 60½" D strips and two 52½" E strips.

Step 4. Sew the D strips to opposite long sides and E strips to the top and bottom of the pieced center; press seams toward D and E strips.

Step 5. Join 32 F rectangles on the 6½" sides in random order to make a side strip; press seams in one direction. Repeat to make a second side strip.

Step 6. Sew a strip to opposite long sides of the pieced center; press seams toward F strips.

Step 7. Repeat Step 5 with two sets of 26 F rectangles to make strips.

Step 8. Sew a Square Dance block to each end of each pieced strip referring to the Placement Diagram for positioning of blocks; press seams toward the blocks.

Step 9. Sew these strips to the top and bottom of the pieced center to complete the pieced top; press seams toward E strips.

Step 10. Layer, quilt, prepare binding and bind edges referring to the Finishing Instructions to finish. ■

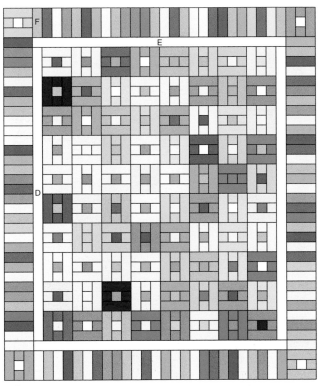

Square Dance
Placement Diagram
64" x 76"

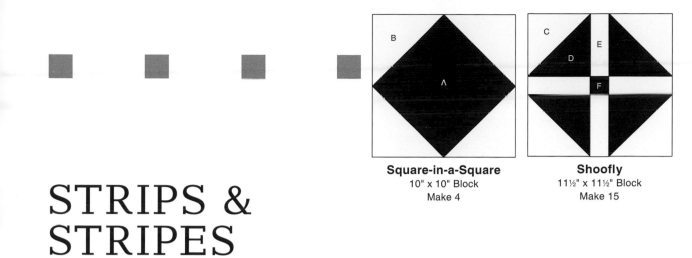

Square-in-a-Square
10" x 10" Block
Make 4

Shoofly
11½" x 11½" Block
Make 15

STRIPS & STRIPES

Design by Johanna Wilson

Set blocks on the diagonal and divide the rows with a stripe fabric to make this bed-size quilt with an antique look.

PROJECT SPECIFICATIONS

Skill Level: Intermediate

Quilt Size: 96¾" x 101¼"

Block Sizes: 10" x 10" and 11½" x 11½"

Number of Blocks: 4 and 15

SUPPLIES

- Batting 103" x 108"
- All-purpose thread to match fabrics
- Quilting thread
- Basic sewing tools and supplies

COMPLETING THE SQUARE-IN-A-SQUARE BLOCKS

Step 1. Mark a diagonal line from corner to corner on the wrong side of each B square.

Step 2. Sew a B square right sides together on opposite corners of A as shown in Figure 1; trim seam to ¼" and press B to the right side.

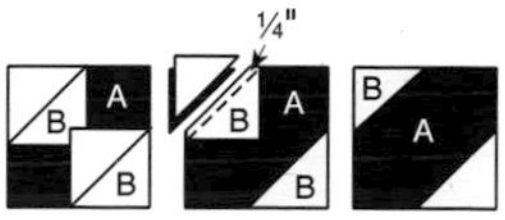

Figure 1

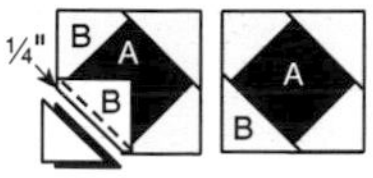

Figure 2

Step 3. Repeat Step 2 with B on the remaining corners of A as shown in Figure 2 to complete one Square-in-a-Square block; repeat to make four blocks.

FABRIC Measurements based on 42" usable fabric width.	#STRIPS/ PIECES	CUT	#PIECES	SUBCUT
⅓ yard each 5 dark prints	1	5⅞" x 42" each fabric	6	5⅞" squares each fabric; cut on 1 diagonal to make 12 D triangles each fabric
	1	2" x 7" F each fabric		
2⅛ yards tan tonal	5	5⅞" x 42" strips	30	5⅞" squares; cut on 1 diagonal to make 60 C triangles
	4	5½" x 42"; set aside 2 strips	30	2" E rectangles
	3	5½" x 42"	16	5½" B squares
2¾ yards rust tonal	3	17½" x 42"	6	17½" squares; cut each square on both diagonals to make 24 G triangles
	2	9" x 42"	6	9" squares; cut each square on 1 diagonal to make 12 H triangles
	10	2¼" x 42" binding		
2½ yards stripe	4	7½" x 81¾" I along length of fabric		
2¾ yards black/ gold print	1	10½" x 42"	4	10½" A squares
	2	10½" x 77¼" K along length of fabric		
	2	10½" x 81¾" J along length of fabric		
Backing		103" x 108"		

COMPLETING THE SHOOFLY BLOCKS

Step 1. Select four same-fabric D triangles and F strip.

Step 2. Sew the F strip between two 5½" x 42" E strips with right sides together along the length; press seams toward F.

Step 3. Subcut the E-F-E strip set into three 2" E-F-E units as shown in Figure 3.

Figure 3

Step 4. Sew C to D to make a C-D unit; press seam toward D. Repeat to make four C-D units.

Step 5. Join two C-D units with E rectangle to make a row as shown in Figure 4; press seams away from E. Repeat to make two rows.

Figure 4   **Figure 5**

Step 6. Join the two rows with an E-F-E unit to complete one Shoofly block as shown in Figure 5; press seams toward the rows. Repeat Steps 1–6 to complete three identical blocks.

Step 7. Repeat Steps 1–6 with remaining pieces and strips to make three Shoofly blocks of each dark fabric combination.

COMPLETING THE QUILT

Step 1. Sew G to opposite sides of nine Shoofly blocks as shown in Figure 6; press seams toward G.

Figure 6   **Figure 7**

Step 2. Sew G to one side and H to two adjacent sides of each remaining block to make corner units as shown in Figure 7; press seams toward H and G.

Step 3. Arrange the pieced units in three rows of five blocks each with two corner units in each row as shown in Figure 8; press seams in one direction.

Figure 8

Step 4. Join the rows with four I strips; press seams toward I strips.

Step 5. Sew J strips to the I sides of the pieced center; press seams toward J strips.

Step 6. Sew a Square-in-a-Square block to each end of each K strip; press seams toward the K strips.

Step 7. Sew a block/K strip to the top and bottom of the pieced center to complete the pieced top; press seams toward the block/K strips.

Step 8. Layer, quilt, prepare binding and bind edges referring to the Finishing Instructions to finish. ∎

Strips & Stripes
Placement Diagram 96¾" x 101¼"

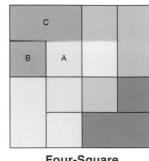

Four-Square
8" x 8" Block
Make 56

FOUR-SQUARE FANTASY

Design by Ruth Swasey

Bring back the psychedelic colors of the 1960s and '70s in this colorful scrappy quilt.

PROJECT SPECIFICATIONS

Skill Level: Beginner

Quilt Size: 80" x 90"

Block Size: 8" x 8"

Number of Blocks: 56

SUPPLIES

- Batting 86" x 96"
- All-purpose thread to match fabrics
- Quilting thread
- Basic sewing tools and supplies

COMPLETING THE BLOCKS

Step 1. Select one A square and two matching B and C pairs.

Step 2. Sew B to opposite sides of A; press seams toward B.

Step 3. Sew C to the remaining sides of A to complete an A-B-C unit as shown in Figure 1; press seams toward C.

FABRIC Measurements based on 42" usable fabric width.	#STRIPS/ PIECES	CUT	#PIECES	SUBCUT
¾ yard yellow print	9	2¼" x 42" binding		
4 yards total bright-color prints	56	5" A squares		
	56	2½" x 5" B rectangle same-fabric pairs (112 B rectangles total)		
	56	2½" x 9" C rectangle same-fabric pairs (112 C rectangles total; match C pairs with B pairs)		
	200	2½" E squares		
3 yards white confetti print	7	8½" x 42"	97	2½" D rectangles
	16	2½" x 42" F/G/H/I		
Backing		86" x 96"		

Step 4. Cut the A-B-C units into four 4½" x 4½" A-B-C units as shown in Figure 2.

Step 5. Repeat Steps 1–4 to complete 224 smaller A-B-C units.

Step 6. Select four different smaller A-B-C units and join as shown in Figure 3 to complete one Four-Square block; press seams in rows in opposite directions. Repeat to make 56 blocks.

Figure 1

4½"
4½"

Figure 2

Figure 3

COMPLETING THE QUILT

Step 1. Select seven blocks and join with six D sashing strips to make a block row; press seams toward D strips. Repeat to make eight block rows.

Step 2. Select six E squares and join with seven D strips to make a sashing row; press seams toward D strips. Repeat to make seven sashing rows.

Step 3. Join the block rows with the sashing rows beginning and ending with a block row to complete the pieced center; press seams toward sashing rows.

Step 4. Join the F/G/H/I strips on short ends with right sides together to make one long strip; press seams open. Subcut strip into two each 78½" F, 72½" G strips, 86½" H and 80½" I strips.

Step 5. Sew F strips to opposite long sides and G strips to the top and bottom of the pieced center; press seams toward the F and G strips.

Step 6. Select and join 41 assorted E squares to make one long strip; press seams in one direction. Repeat to make two long strips. Repeat with 38 E squares to make shorter strips for the top and bottom.

Step 7. Sew the longer E strips to opposite long sides of the pieced center; press seams toward F strips. Repeat with the shorter E strips on the top and bottom of the pieced center; press seams toward G strips.

Four-Square Fantasy
Placement Diagram 80" x 90"

Step 8. Sew H strips to opposite long sides and I strips to the top and bottom of the pieced center; press seams toward H and I strips to complete the pieced top.

Step 9. Layer, quilt, prepare binding and bind edges referring to the Finishing Instructions. ▪

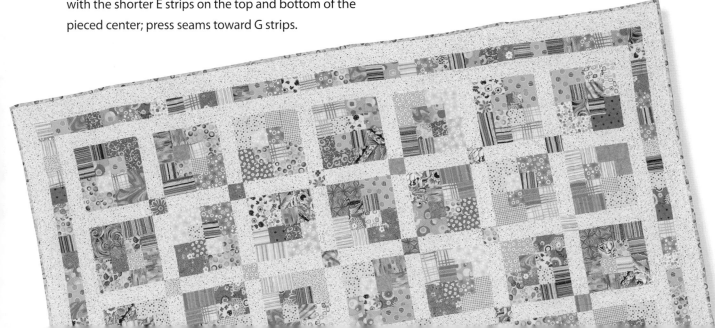

QUILTING FOR CHRISTMAS MAKES THE HOLIDAY EXTRA SPECIAL

Nothing compares to handmade holiday gifts or decorations. Whether you choose to make a place mat, ornaments or a neat bag, your efforts won't go unnoticed by friends or family who gather at your home during this magical time of the year.

MERRY CHRISTMAS BAG

Design by Sandra L. Hatch

Carry your Merry Christmas bag to the mall
or fill it with gifts for a family this holiday.

PROJECT SPECIFICATIONS

Skill Level: Beginner
Bag Size: 18" x 21"

SUPPLIES

- Batting 24" x 39" and 1" x 44"
- Red and green all-purpose thread to match fabrics
- ¼ yard stick-on tear-off fabric stabilizer
- Basting spray
- Basic sewing tools and supplies

FABRIC Measurements based on 42" usable fabric width.	#STRIPS/PIECES	CUT
⅛ yard green print	2	1½" x 42" D
¼ yard cream tonal	1	2½" x 36½" E
	2	1" x 36½" F
¾ yard red holly check	1	14" x 36½" A rectangle for bag bottom
	1	3" x 42" B
	1	3" x 42" strip for handles
⅞ yard tan print	2	1½" x 42" C strips
	1	21½" x 36½" lining

COMPLETING THE BAG TOP

Step 1. Cut fabric-stabilizer strips to fit E; adhere strips to the wrong side of the E strip.

Step 2. Prepare your sewing machine for a chosen embroidery design or message. ***Note:*** *The design used for this project included a written message and a line of a built-in embroidery design above and below the message.*

Step 3. Stitch the chosen embroidery designs onto the strip. ***Note:*** *You may embroider part of the design now and part of it during the quilting process, if desired.*

Step 4. When embroidery is complete, remove fabric stabilizer.

Step 5. Sew a C strip to a D strip to make a C-D strip set; press seam toward D. Repeat to make two C-D strip sets.

Step 6. Subcut the C-D strip sets into (36) 1½" C-D units as shown in Figure 1.

Figure 1

Step 7. Join 18 C-D units to make a strip as shown in Figure 2; press seams toward D.

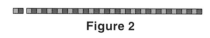

Figure 2

Step 8. Sew a C-D strip to opposite sides of E as shown in Figure 3; press seams toward the C-D strips.

Figure 3

Step 9. Sew an F strip to each long side of the pieced strip to complete the pieced band as shown in Figure 4; press seams toward F.

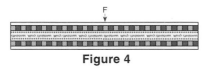
Figure 4

Step 10. Sew A to the bottom and B to the top of the pieced band to complete the bag top as shown in Figure 5; press seams toward A and B pieces.

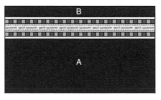
Figure 5

Step 11. Apply basting spray to the batting; lay the completed bag top right side up on the batting.

Step 12. Machine-quilt in the ditch of the seams of the pieced band and as desired on the A and B pieces.

Step 13. When quilting is complete, trim batting edges even with the completed bag top.

MAKING HANDLES

Step 1. Remove the selvage edge from each end of the handle strip. Cut into two equal-length strips.

Step 2. Fold one long edge of each handle strip ¼" to the wrong side and press.

Step 3. Fold over opposite long edge of each strip 1" as shown in Figure 6 and press; fold the pressed ¼" edge over ¾" on top of the raw edge of the pressed 1" edge and press.

1"
Figure 6

Step 4. Open the pressed edges of each strip and insert the 1"-wide batting strip, aligning batting strip with pressed lines as shown in Figure 7.

Figure 7

Step 5. Refold pressed edges over the batting, first folding over the 1" edges and overlapping with the ¾" folded edges; press to make 1"-wide strips.

Step 6. Stitch along folded-over edge along center of strips as shown in Figure 8.

Figure 8

Step 7. Square-up ends of each strip to complete handles.

ATTACHING HANDLES

Step 1. Fold the quilted bag top in half, matching embroidered strip ends, and lay on a flat surface.

Step 2. Measure in 3¾" from the side raw edge and pin the right side of one end of one handle to the top right side edge of the bag as shown in Figure 9. Measure in 3½" from the folded edge and pin the opposite end of the same handle right sides together with bag top edge, again referring to Figure 9. ***Note:*** *The right side of the handle strip is the side without the overlapped edge.*

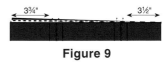
Figure 9

Step 3. Turn folded bag top over, align and pin the second handle even with the ends of the handle pinned in Step 2 as shown in Figure 10.

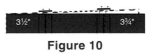
Figure 10

Step 4. Machine-stitch over ends of handles several times ⅛" from edge to secure in place as shown in Figure 11.

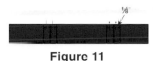

Figure 11

COMPLETING THE BAG

Step 1. Lay the quilted bag top on the previously cut lining piece; trim lining to fit the quilted top, if necessary.

Step 2. Place lining piece right sides together with quilted top. Stitch across top edge of bag, stitching over handle ends.

Step 3. Press seam toward lining and topstitch close to seam on lining side as shown in Figure 12.

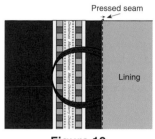

Figure 12

Step 4. Fold bag top and lining sections with right sides together as shown in Figure 13. Starting at the bag bottom corner, stitch all around bag top and lining, leaving a 6" opening in the bottom edge of the lining, again referring to Figure 13.

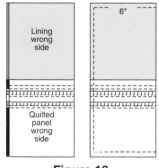

Figure 13

Step 5. Trim corners of bag top and lining, and trim batting close to seam at top side edge and along bottom corners to reduce bulk.

Step 6. Turn right side out through opening in lining, making sure corners are completely turned.

Merry Christmas Bag
Placement Diagram
18" x 21"

Step 7. Press seam inside at lining opening edges and machine-stitch opening closed close to edges as shown in Figure 14.

Figure 14

Step 8. Before inserting lining inside bag, press side seam of bag to help make bag lie flat at sides when complete.

Step 9. Insert lining inside bag. Press lining to the inside at the top edge of the bag. Insert iron inside bag and press lining flat as far inside as the iron will slide. Hold the top side of the bag and insert your hand inside the bag to the corners to be sure lining is completely inside and aligned at corners.

Step 10. Topstitch along top edge of bag ¼"–⅜" from edge using matching all-purpose thread.

Step 11. Choose another area on the bag band and topstitch to hold lining layer and bag top together. **Note:** *This may be in the seam of a strip or ¼" from a seam or in the center of a strip.* ∎

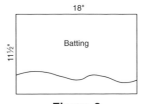

HAPPY SNOWMEN PLACE MAT

Design by Connie Rand

These silly snowmen will bring a few smiles to your holiday table.

PROJECT SPECIFICATIONS

Skill Level: Beginner

Place Mat Size: 17½" x 11"

SUPPLIES

- Batting 18" x 11½"
- All-purpose thread to match fabrics
- ½ yard white medium-weight fusible interfacing
- ½ yard fusible web
- 3 green, 6 blue and 6 red round sequins
- 4 red flat snowflake sequins
- 3 gold flat star sequins
- Black permanent pen
- Basic sewing tools and supplies

APPLIQUÉ CUTTING

Step 1. Apply white medium-weight fusible interfacing to the wrong side of all white tonals to prevent shadows of dark fabric.

Step 2. Trace appliqué shapes on paper side of fusible web referring to patterns for number to cut; cut out, leaving a margin around each piece.

Step 3. Fuse shapes to the wrong side of fabrics, referring to patterns for fabric colors. Cut along traced lines; remove paper backing.

FABRIC Measurements based on 42" usable fabric width.	#STRIPS/PIECES	CUT
Scraps of red, green and orange prints or tonals		Appliqué pieces as per patterns
¼ yard total light blue tonals	12-14	varying-width x 20"
¼ yard total white tonals		Appliqué pieces as per patterns
¼ yard light blue swirl	2	2¼" x 42" binding
Backing		19" x 13"

PIECING THE PLACE MAT

Step 1. Cut the blue tonal strips at an angle from one end of a strip to the other as shown in Figure 1.

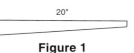

20"

Figure 1

Step 2. Place the snow appliqué pattern piece on the batting and mark the top of the snow, referring to Figure 2. ***Note:*** *The patterns given have been reversed for fusible appliqué. Flip the snow pattern before placing it on the batting.*

18"

11½"

Batting

Figure 2

Step 3. Place a blue strip on the batting right side up, making sure that it will be under the top of the snow piece.

Step 4. Place another blue strip on the first strip right sides together, aligning raw edges; stitch ¼" from the raw edge as shown in Figure 3.

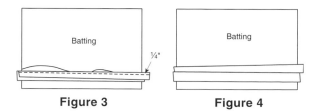

Figure 3   **Figure 4**

Step 5. Flip the second strip up and finger-press it in place as shown in Figure 4.

Step 6. Continue adding strips until the batting is covered referring to Figure 5; trim excess fabric even with edges of batting.

Figure 5

Step 7. Arrange snowman and tree shapes on background referring to Placement Diagram for positioning and motif patterns for numerical order of placement; fuse in place.

Step 8. Place the snow piece on the bottom of the background piece with bottom edges aligned; fuse in place.

Step 9. Place backing right side down on a flat surface with batting on top; center the pieced

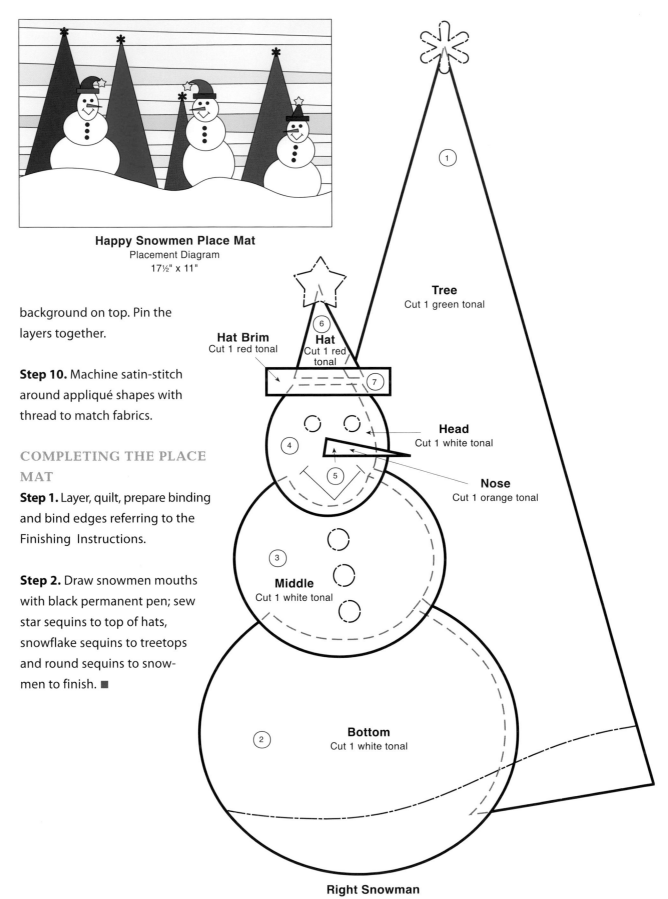

Happy Snowmen Place Mat
Placement Diagram
17½" x 11"

background on top. Pin the
layers together.

Step 10. Machine satin-stitch
around appliqué shapes with
thread to match fabrics.

COMPLETING THE PLACE MAT

Step 1. Layer, quilt, prepare binding
and bind edges referring to the
Finishing Instructions.

Step 2. Draw snowmen mouths
with black permanent pen; sew
star sequins to top of hats,
snowflake sequins to treetops
and round sequins to snowmen to finish. ■

Tree
Cut 1 green tonal

Hat Brim
Cut 1 red tonal

Hat
Cut 1 red tonal

Head
Cut 1 white tonal

Nose
Cut 1 orange tonal

Middle
Cut 1 white tonal

Bottom
Cut 1 white tonal

Right Snowman

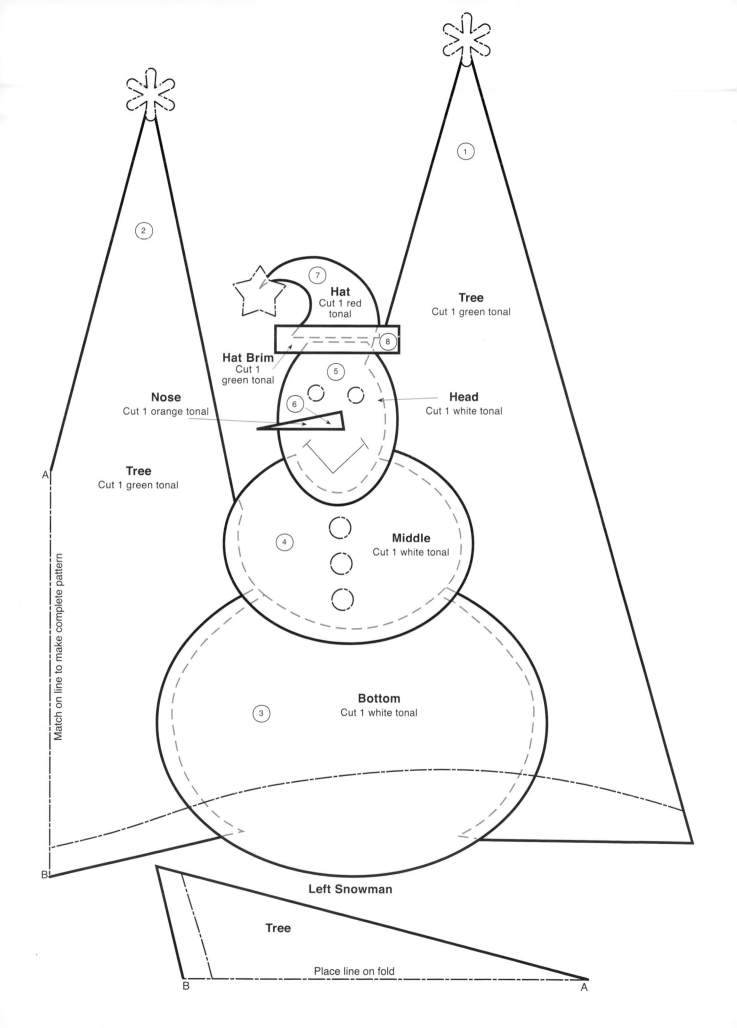

Tree
Cut 1 green tonal

①

Tree
Cut 1 green tonal

②

Hat
Cut 1 red
tonal

⑦

Hat Brim
Cut 1
green tonal

⑧

Nose
Cut 1 orange tonal

⑥

Head
Cut 1 white tonal

⑤

Tree
Cut 1 green tonal

Middle
Cut 1 white tonal

④

Bottom
Cut 1 white tonal

③

Match on line to make complete pattern

A

B

Left Snowman

Tree

Place line on fold

B

A

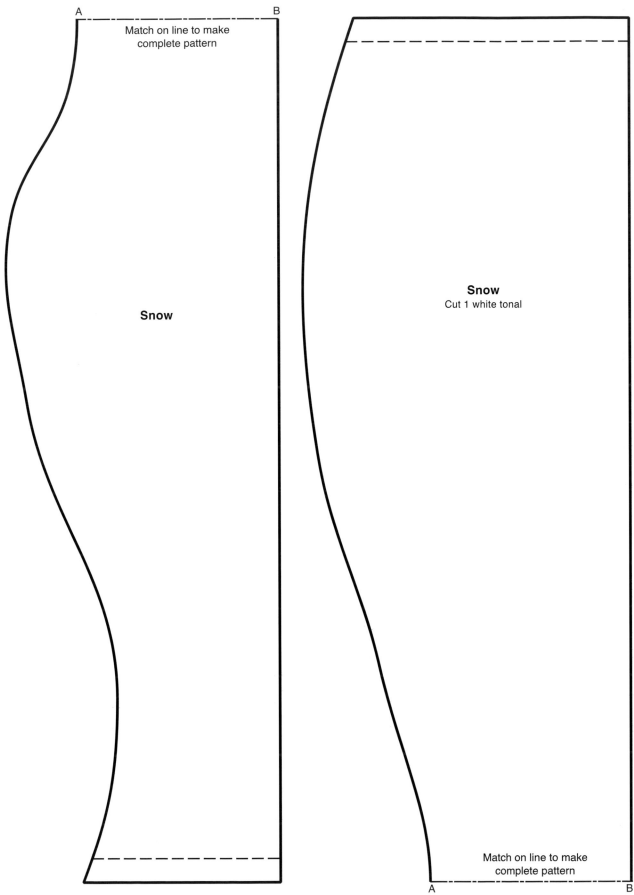

A   B

Match on line to make
complete pattern

Snow

Snow
Cut 1 white tonal

Match on line to make
complete pattern

A   B

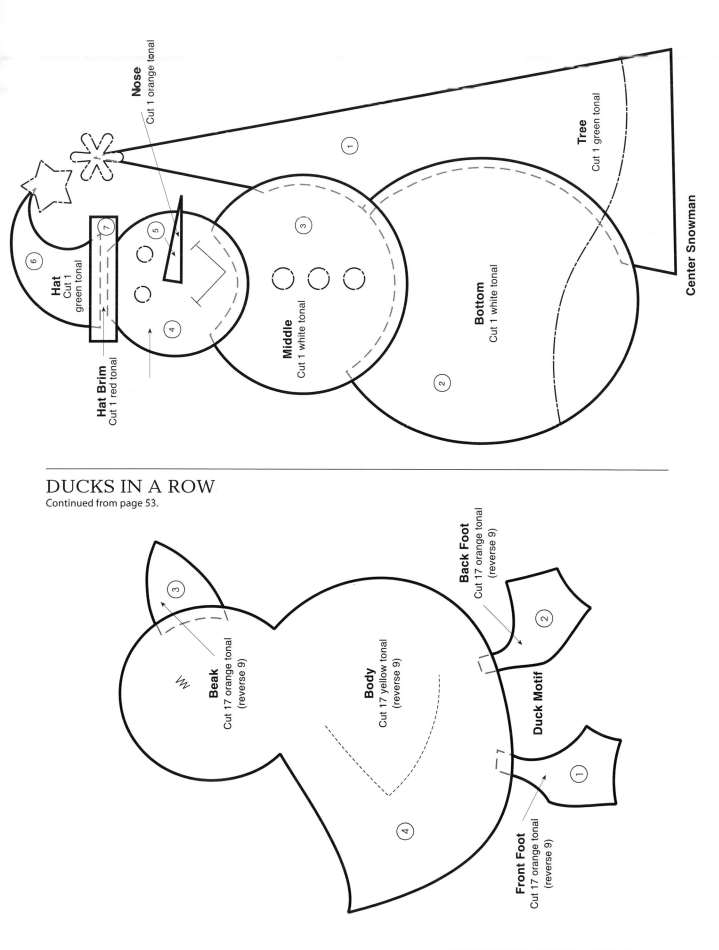

Nose
Cut 1 orange tonal

Tree
Cut 1 green tonal

Center Snowman

Hat
Cut 1
green tonal

Hat Brim
Cut 1 red tonal

Middle
Cut 1 white tonal

Bottom
Cut 1 white tonal

DUCKS IN A ROW

Continued from page 53.

Beak
Cut 17 orange tonal
(reverse 9)

Body
Cut 17 yellow tonal
(reverse 9)

Back Foot
Cut 17 orange tonal
(reverse 9)

Duck Motif

Front Foot
Cut 17 orange tonal
(reverse 9)

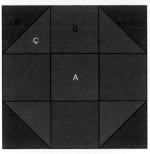

Churn Dash
12" x 12" Block
Make 1

CHRISTMAS HOLLY PLACE MAT

Design by Barbara A. Clayton

Piece a 12"-square block and add holly-leaf appliqué motifs to strips on each side to make a quick holiday place mat.

PROJECT SPECIFICATIONS

Skill Level: Beginner

Place Mat Size: 18" x 12"

Block Size: 12" x 12"

Number of Blocks: 1

SUPPLIES

- Batting 19" x 13"
- All-purpose thread to match fabrics
- Clear nylon monofilament for quilting
- ⅜ yard fusible web
- 2 (3" x 12") strips fabric stabilizer
- Basic sewing tools and supplies

APPLIQUÉ

Step 1. Trace appliqué shapes given onto the paper side of the fusible web; cut out fabrics, leaving a margin around each one.

Step 2. Fuse the shapes to the wrong side of the fabrics as directed on each piece for color. Cut out shapes on traced lines; remove paper backing.

Step 3. Arrange two holly leaf motifs on each E strip in numerical order referring to Figure 1, overlapping as necessary. When satisfied with placement, fuse shapes in place.

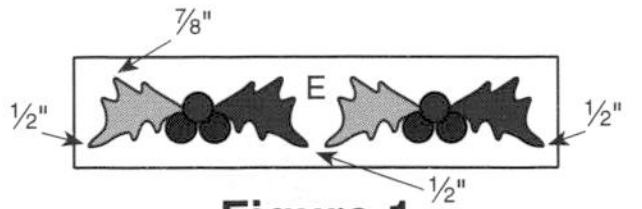

FABRIC Measurements based on 42" usable fabric width.	#STRIPS/ PIECES	CUT	#PIECES	SUBCUT
⅛ yard each dark and medium green tonals		Appliqué pieces as per patterns		
¼ yard green print 1	1	4½" A square		
	2	4⅞" squares		Cut in half on 1 diagonal to make 4 C triangles
¼ yard cream tonal	2	3½" x 12½" E		
¼ yard red mottled	4	4½" B squares Appliqué pieces as per patterns		
¼ yard red tonal	2	4⅞" squares		Cut in half on 1 diagonal to make 4 D triangles
		Appliqué pieces as per patterns		
¼ yard green print 2	2	2¼" x 42" binding		
Backing		19" x 13"		

Figure 1

Step 4. Pin fabric stabilizer strips to the wrong side of each fused E strip.

Step 5. Using thread to match fabrics, machine zig-zag-stitch around the edge of each fused piece and

along the detail line on each leaf to hold in place; remove fabric stabilizer.

COMPLETING THE BLOCK

Step 1. Sew B to opposite sides of A to make the center row; press seams toward B.

Step 2. Sew C to D along the diagonal to make a C-D unit; press seam toward D. Repeat to make four C-D units.

Step 3. Sew a C-D unit to opposite sides of B as shown in Figure 2; press seams toward B. Repeat to make two B-C-D rows.

Figure 2

Step 4. Sew a B-C-D row to opposite sides of the center row referring to the block drawing to complete one Churn Dash block; press seams away from the center row.

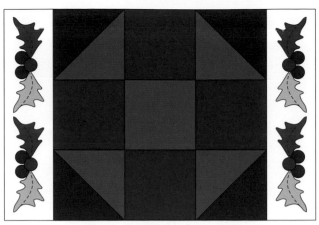

Christmas Holly Place Mat
Placement Diagram 18" x 12"

COMPLETING THE TOP

Step 1. Sew an appliquéd E strip to opposite sides of the Churn Dash block; press seams toward E.

Step 2. Layer, quilt, prepare binding and bind edges referring to the Finishing Instructions.

Step 3. Hand- or machine-quilt as desired to finish. *Note: The project shown was machine-quilted using clear nylon monofilament around the appliqué motifs and using thread to match fabrics in the block.* ■

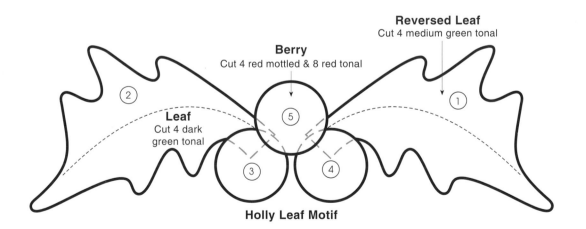

Reversed Leaf
Cut 4 medium green tonal

Berry
Cut 4 red mottled & 8 red tonal

Leaf
Cut 4 dark green tonal

Holly Leaf Motif

BEADED PATCHWORK ORNAMENTS

Design by Chris Malone

Beads add elegance to some simple patchwork ornaments.

PROJECT SPECIFICATIONS

Skill Level: Beginner

Bell Ornament Size: Approximately 5" x 5"

Ball Ornament Size: 5¼" x 5¾"

Tree Ornament Size: 5" x 6½"

SUPPLIES

- 3 (7" x 7") squares and scraps fleece or needled polyester batting
- All-purpose thread to match fabrics
- Quilting thread
- 3 (24") lengths ⅜"-wide gold wire-edge ribbon
- Assortment of coordinating 3–10mm glass beads
- Beeswax
- Basic sewing tools and supplies

FABRIC Measurements based on 42" usable fabric width.	#STRIPS/ PIECES	CUT
4 red scraps with metallic highlights	1	1¾" x 6"
	1	1½" x 6"
	2	2" x 6"
	1	6" x 6"
2" x 3" scrap gold metallic		
4 green scraps with metallic highlights	1	1¾" x 6"
	2	1½" x 6"
	1	2" x 6"
	1	6" x 6"
2" x 5" scrap brown mottled		
Scraps brown, cream, black and tan with metallic highlights	1	1½" x 6" brown
	1	1½" x 6" tan
	1	2" x 6" black
	1	2¼" x 6" cream
	1	6" x 6" tan

COMPLETING THE TREE ORNAMENT

Step 1. Join the green scrap strips along the 6" length to make a rectangle as shown in Figure 1; press seams in one direction.

1¾" x 6"
1½" x 6"
1½" x 6"
2" x 6"

Figure 1

Step 2. Trace the tree pattern given onto the wrong side of the 6" x 6" square green scrap; place right sides together with the pieced rectangle.

Step 3. Pin the layered section to one 7" x 7" fleece or batting square; stitch all around on traced lines, leaving opening at bottom as marked on pattern.

Step 4. Cut out; trim batting close to seam and clip corners. Turn right side out and press flat.

Step 5. Repeat Steps 2–4 with the tree trunk piece on 2" x 5" scrap brown mottled and a scrap of fleece or batting, leaving one short end open.

Step 6. Insert trunk piece into the opening, fold opening seam to the inside and hand-stitch opening closed, catching trunk piece in the stitches.

Step 7. Machine-stitch in the ditch of seams.

Step 8. Hand-stitch red beads randomly over the front side of the tree. ***Note:*** *Run threads used for beading through the beeswax to add additional strength.*

Step 9. Anchor a doubled thread at one bottom corner of the trunk; string on about six glass beads and end with a 3mm bead, making a 1" dangle. Skipping the last bead on the string, insert the needle back through the other beads and into the fabric. Adjust the tension of the dangle by holding onto the last

bead while pulling on the thread. Knot the thread; move the needle to the other corner and repeat the dangle. Knot the thread; make a third dangle in the center. Knot and clip the thread.

Step 10. Repeat to add a 10mm bead and 3mm bead to the top of the tree.

Step 11. Fold one 24" length of ribbon in half and tie a knot about 4" from the end of the loop. Tie the free ends in a bow.

Step 12. Tack the ribbon hanger to the top back of the ornament. Trim the ends as needed; tie a knot at each end.

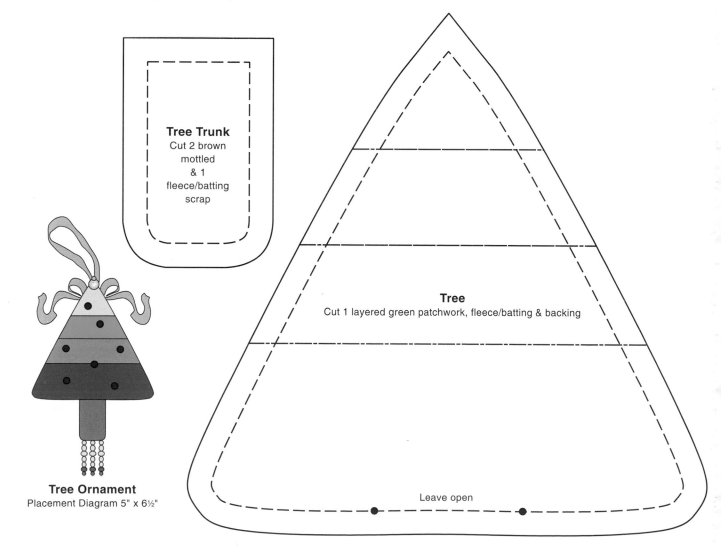

Tree Trunk
Cut 2 brown mottled & 1 fleece/batting scrap

Tree
Cut 1 layered green patchwork, fleece/batting & backing

Leave open

Tree Ornament
Placement Diagram 5" x 6½"

COMPLETING THE BALL ORNAMENT

Step 1. Repeat Steps 1–7 for Tree Ornament to complete the Ball Ornament using the red scrap strips and square, and the ball ornament pattern, referring to Figure 2. Repeat instructions with the gold metallic scrap and ball-cap pattern.

| 1¾" x 6" |
| 1½" x 6" |
| 2" x 6" |
| 2" x 6" |

Figure 2

Step 2. Hand-stitch glass beads across the second band of the ball ornament. ***Note:*** *The sample has five sets of five 3mm beads each with a ¼" space between the sets.*

Step 3. Anchor a doubled thread at the bottom tip of the ornament; string on about five larger glass beads and then a smaller (3mm) bead at the end, making a 1¾" dangle.

Step 4. Skipping the last bead on the string, insert the needle back through the other beads and into the fabric. Adjust the tension of the dangle by holding onto the last bead while pulling on the thread; knot and clip the thread.

Step 5. Repeat Steps 11 and 12 for tree ornament to make ribbon hanger.

Ball Ornament
Placement Diagram 5¼" x 5¾"

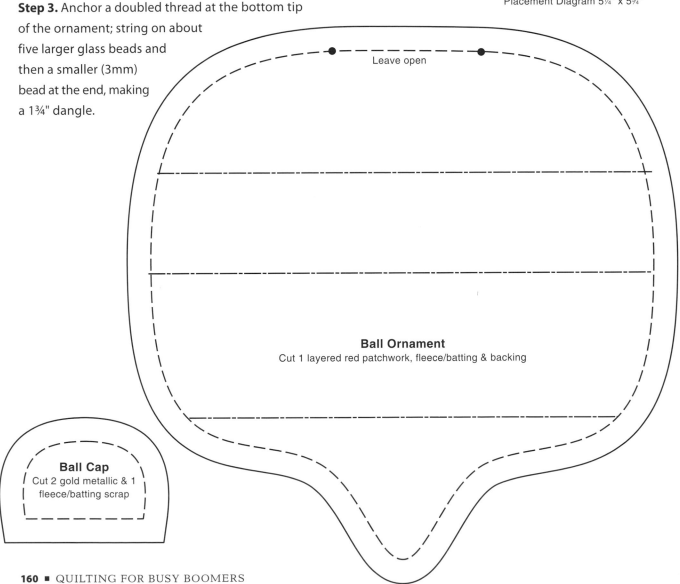

Leave open

Ball Ornament
Cut 1 layered red patchwork, fleece/batting & backing

Ball Cap
Cut 2 gold metallic & 1 fleece/batting scrap

COMPLETING THE BELL ORNAMENT

Step 1. Repeat Steps 1–7 for tree ornament to complete the bell ornament using the black, brown, tan and cream strips, tan square and the bell ornament pattern and referring to Figure 3.

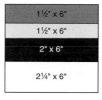

Figure 3

Step 2. Hand-sew glass beads across the second band of the bell ornament. **Note:** The model has two or three 3mm gold beads alternating with single 6mm black beads placed about ³⁄₁₆" between sets.

Step 3. Anchor a doubled thread on the center bottom of the bell. String on about five beads and end with a 3mm bead, making a 1½" dangle. Skipping the last bead on the string, insert the needle back through the other beads and into the fabric. Adjust the tension of the dangle by holding onto the last bead while pulling on the thread. Knot and clip the thread.

Step 4. Repeat Steps 11 and 12 for Tree Ornament to make ribbon hanger. ■

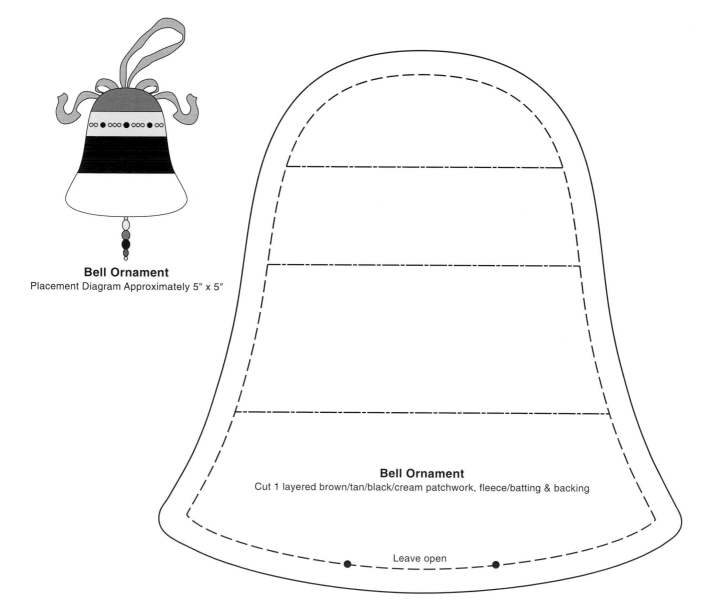

Bell Ornament
Placement Diagram Approximately 5" x 5"

Bell Ornament
Cut 1 layered brown/tan/black/cream patchwork, fleece/batting & backing

Leave open

SHIMMERING SNOWFLAKES

Design by Jill Reber

Silver metallic fabrics shine in this patchwork Christmas stocking.

PROJECT SPECIFICATIONS

Skill Level: Beginner
Stocking Size: 10" x 15½"

SUPPLIES

- 18½" x 21½" rectangle batting
- All-purpose thread to match fabrics
- Quilting thread
- 1¼ yards ⅜"-wide silver metallic wire-edged ribbon
- 1 (¾") silver bell
- Basting spray
- Basic sewing tools and supplies

COMPLETING THE STOCKING

Step 1. Sew a B strip to a C strip with right sides together along the length; press seams toward C strips. Repeat to make two B-C strip sets.

Step 2. Subcut the B-C strip sets into (21) 3½" B-C units as shown in Figure 1.

Figure 1

Step 3. Join three A squares and three B-C units to make a row as shown in Figure 2; press seams toward A. Repeat to make seven rows.

FABRIC Measurements based on 42" usable fabric width.	#STRIPS/PIECES	CUT	#PIECES	SUBCUT
¼ yard white-with-silver metallic snowflakes	2	2" x 42" B		
¼ yard blue tonal	2	2" x 42" C		
⅜ yard blue metallic print	2 1	3½" x 42" 3" x 42" binding	21	3½" A squares
⅝ yard white tonal for lining	1	18½" x 21½" rectangle		

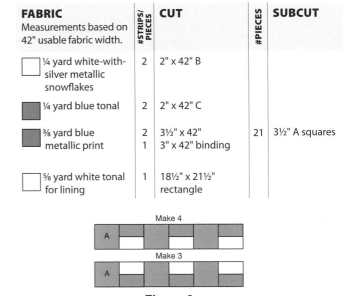

Make 4

Make 3

Figure 2

Step 4. Join the rows to complete an 18½" x 21½" patchwork rectangle as shown in Figure 3.

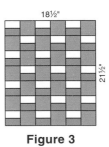

18½"

21½"

Figure 3

Step 5. Lay the 18½" x 21½" lining piece wrong side up on a flat surface; spray-baste the batting and lay it

on top. Spray-baste the wrong side of the patchwork rectangle and lay it right side up on the batting.

Step 6. Prepare the stocking pattern using pattern given; lay the pattern on the patchwork rectangle as shown in Figure 4; mark and cut out.

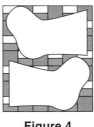

Figure 4

Step 7. Stitch around edges of patchwork stockings to hold the layers together.

Step 8. With right sides together, pin and stitch stocking edges together, leaving top edge open and stopping stitching 8" from the top edge of the heel side of the stocking.

Step 9. Clip curves, turn right side out.

Step 10. Press the 3"-wide binding strip in half with wrong sides together along the length.

Step 11. Leaving a 6" extension, sew the binding strip to the top inside lining edge of the stocking.

Step 12. Press the binding strip up and away from the lining; fold down over the right side of the stocking, enclosing the raw edge of the extension inside the fold as shown in Figure 5.

Figure 5

Step 13. Machine-topstitch the binding to the stocking and through the extension edges as shown in Figure 6.

Figure 6

Step 14. Turn the stocking wrong side out again.

Step 15. Fold the extension piece to form a loop on the outside, tucking raw edge into the open seam; complete the seam stitching.

Step 16. Tie the ribbon into a multiple-loop bow and hand-stitch it and the bell to the loop edge of the stocking to finish. ■

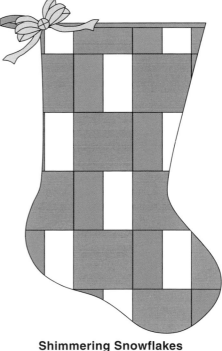

Shimmering Snowflakes
Placement Diagram 10" x 15½"

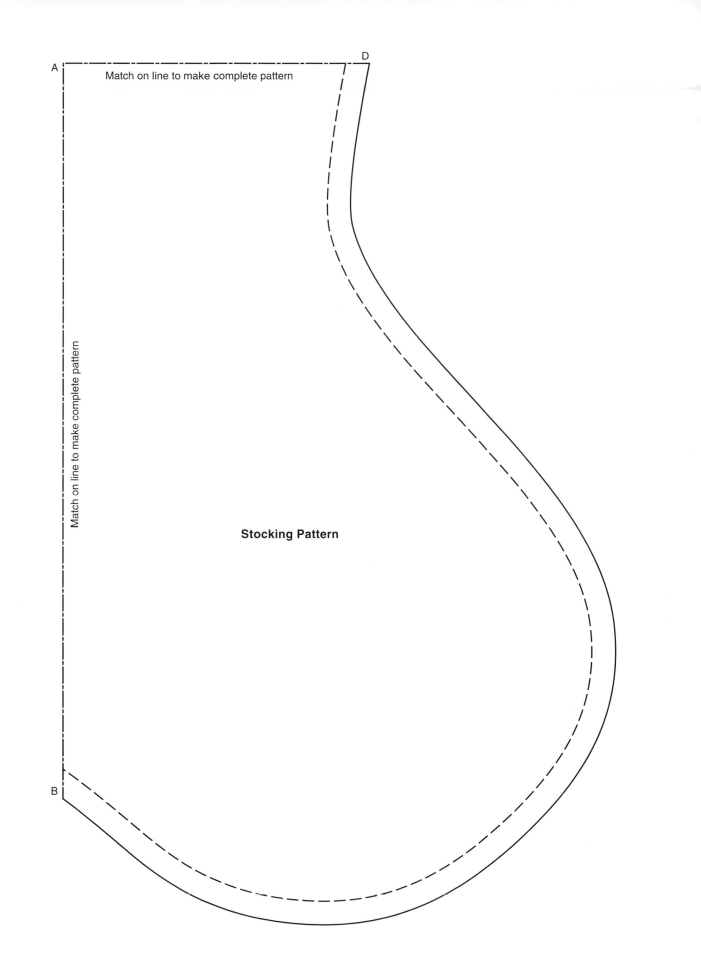

A

Match on line to make complete pattern

Match on line to make complete pattern

D

Stocking Pattern

B

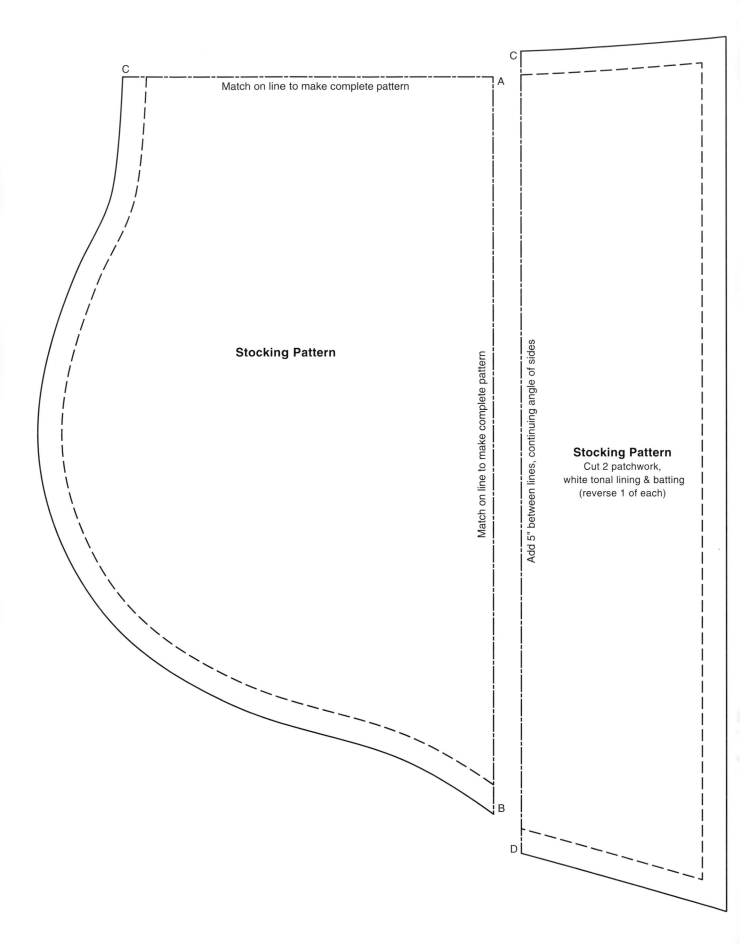

Stocking Pattern

Match on line to make complete pattern

Match on line to make complete pattern

Add 5" between lines, continuing angle of sides

Stocking Pattern
Cut 2 patchwork,
white tonal lining & batting
(reverse 1 of each)

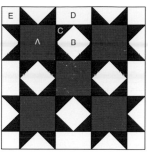

Twinkle Stars
16" x 16" Block
Make 5

TWINKLE, TWINKLE CHRISTMAS STARS

Design by Julie Weaver

Add sparkle to your Christmas with this striking throw.

PROJECT SPECIFICATIONS

Skill Level: Beginner

Quilt Size: 60¼" x 60¼"

Block Size: 16" x 16"

Number of Blocks: 5

SUPPLIES

- Batting 66" x 66"
- All-purpose thread to match fabrics
- Quilting thread
- Basic sewing tools and supplies

COMPLETING THE BLOCKS

Step 1. Draw a diagonal line from corner to corner on the wrong side of each C square. Referring to Figure 1, place C on opposite corners of B; stitch on the marked lines. Trim seam to ¼"; press C to the right side.

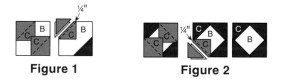

Figure 1

Figure 2

Step 2. Repeat on the remaining corners of B to complete one B-C unit as shown in Figure 2. Repeat to make 20 B-C units.

Step 3. Repeat Step 1 with C on both ends of D referring to Figure 3 to complete 40 C-D units.

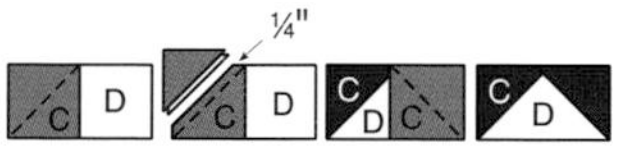

FABRIC Measurements based on 42" usable fabric width.	#STRIPS/ PIECES	CUT	#PIECES	SUBCUT
1⅛ yards red tonal	10	2½" x 42"	160	2½" C squares
	5	1½" x 42" H/I		
1¼ yards cream tonal	7	4½" x 42"	20	4½" B squares
			60	2½" D rectangles
	2	2½" x 42"	20	2½" E squares
1½ yards black lengthwise stripe	8	6" x 42" identical L strips		
2⅜ yards black print	3	4½" x 42"	25	4½" A squares
	1	23⅞" square; cut on both diagonals to make 4 F triangles		
	2	12¼" squares; cut on 1 diagonal to make 4 G triangles		
	5	1½" x 42" J/K		
	7	2¼" x 42" binding		
Backing		66" x 66"		

Figure 3

Figure 4

Step 4. To complete one block, arrange and join two D rectangles, two B-C units and one A square to complete the center row referring to Figure 4; press seams toward A and D.

Step 5. Arrange and join one B-C unit, two C-D units and two A squares to make an A row referring to Figure 5;

press seams toward A. Repeat to make two A rows.

Step 6. Join one D rectangle, two E squares and two C-D units to make a top row referring to Figure 6; press seams toward D and E. Repeat to make a bottom row.

Step 7. Arrange and join the rows as shown in Figure 7 to complete one Twinkle Stars block; press seams toward the A rows. Repeat to make five blocks.

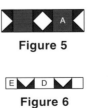

Figure 5

Figure 6

Figure 7

COMPLETING THE QUILT

Step 1. Join three blocks with two G triangles to make the center diagonal row as shown in Figure 8;

press seams in one direction and toward G.

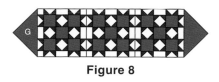

Figure 8

Step 2. Sew F to two opposite sides and G to one remaining side of one block to make a corner unit as shown in Figure 9; press seams toward F and G. Repeat to make two corner units.

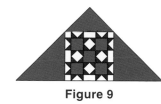

Figure 9

Step 3. Sew a corner unit to opposite sides of the center diagonal row to complete the pieced center referring to the Placement Diagram; press seams toward the corner units.

Step 4. Join the H/I strips on short ends to make one long strip; press seams open. Subcut strip into two 45¾" H strips and two 47¾" I strips.

Step 5. Join the J/K strips on short ends to make one long strip; press seams open. Subcut strip into two 47¾" J strips and two 49¾" K strips.

Step 6. Join two L strips on short ends to make one long strip; press seam open. Repeat to make four strips. Trim strips to make four 64" L strips. **Note:** If you want to match the stripes at the mitered corners, you will need four identical L strips.

Step 7. Sew H strips to opposite sides and I strips to the top and bottom of the pieced center; press seams toward H and I strips.

Step 8. Sew J strips to opposite sides and K strips to the top and bottom of the pieced center; press seams toward J and K strips.

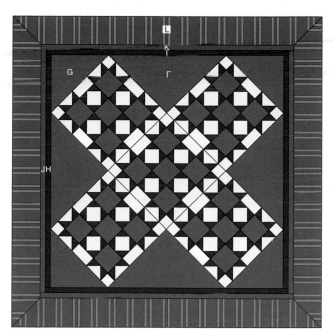

Twinkle, Twinkle Christmas Stars
Placement Diagram
60¼" x 60¼"

Step 9. Center and sew an L strip to each side of the pieced center, stopping stitching ¼" from each end as shown in Figure 10; press seams toward L strips.

Figure 10   **Figure 11**

Step 10. Fold one strip on each corner under to form a 45-degree angle as shown in Figure 11; press to make a creased line.

Step 11. Fold the quilted top on the diagonal and stitch on the creased lines to extend the angle to make a mitered corner as shown in Figure 12.

Figure 12   **Figure 13**

Step 12. Trim seam to ¼" and press mitered seam open as shown in Figure 13 to complete the pieced top.

Step 13. Layer, quilt, prepare binding and bind edges referring to the Finishing Instructions to finish. ■

FINISHING INSTRUCTIONS

FINISHING THE TOP

Adding Borders

Borders are an integral part of the quilt and should complement the colors and designs used in the quilt center. Borders frame a quilt just like a mat and frame do a picture.

Border strips may be mitered or butted at the corners as shown in Figures 1 and 2.

Figure 1   Figure 2

Butted Border Strips

1. To determine the size for butted border strips, measure across the center of the completed quilt top from the top raw edge to the bottom raw edge. This measurement will include a ¼" seam allowance.

2. Cut two border strips that length by the chosen width of the border.

3. Sew these strips to the opposite sides of the pieced center referring to Figure 3. Press the seam allowance toward border strips.

Figure 3

4. Measure across the completed quilt top at the center, from one side raw edge to the other side raw edge, including the two border strips added.

5. Cut two border strips that length by the chosen width of the border.

6. Sew a strip to the top and bottom, again referring to Figure 3. Press the seams toward border strips.

Mitered Border Strips

1. To make mitered corners, measure across the center of the completed quilt top. To this add twice the width of the border and ½" for seam allowances to determine the length of the strips. Repeat for opposite sides.

2. Center and sew on each strip, stopping stitching ¼" from each corner and leaving the remainder of the strip dangling as shown in Figure 4.

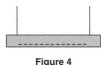

Figure 4

3. Referring to Figures 5–7 for steps 3–5, press corners at a 45-degree angle to form a crease.

4. Align border strips right sides together; stitch from the inside quilt corner to the outside on the creased line.

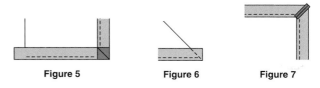

Figure 5   Figure 6   Figure 7

5. Trim excess away after stitching and press mitered seams open.

6. Carefully press the entire piece, including the pieced center. Avoid pulling and stretching while pressing.

COMPLETING YOUR QUILT

Choosing a Quilting Design

There are several types of quilting designs, some of which may not have to be marked. The easiest of the unmarked designs is in-the-ditch quilting. Here the quilting stitches are

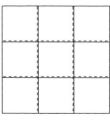

Figure 8

placed in the valley created by the seams joining two pieces together, or next to the edge of an appliqué design. Machine quilters choose this option because the stitches are not as obvious on the finished quilt (Figure 8).

Outline-quilting ¼" or more away from seams or appliqué shapes is another no-mark alternative (Figure 9) that prevents having to sew through the layers made by seams, thus making stitching easier.

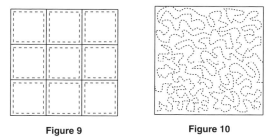

Figure 9   Figure 10

Meander or free-motion quilting by machine (Figure 10) fills in open spaces and doesn't require marking. It is fun and easy to stitch.

Marking the Top for Quilting

If you choose a fancy or allover design for quilting, you will need to transfer the design to your quilt top before layering with the backing and batting.

Use a sharp medium-lead or silver pencil on light background fabrics. Test the pencil marks to guarantee that they will wash out of your quilt top when quilting is complete, or be sure your quilting stitches cover the pencil marks. Mechanical pencils with very fine points may be used successfully to mark quilts.

Manufactured quilting-design templates are available in many designs and sizes, and are cut out of a durable plastic template material that is easy to use.

No matter what marking method you use, remember—the marked lines should never show on the finished quilt. When the top is marked, it is ready for layering.

Preparing the Quilt Backing

A backing is generally cut at least 6" larger than the quilt top or 3" larger on all sides. For a 64" x 78" finished quilt, the backing would need to be at least 70" x 84".

To avoid having the seam down the center of the back, cut two fabric pieces the length of the backing needed; cut or tear one of these pieces in half, and sew half to each side of the second piece as shown in Figure 11.

Quilt backings that are more than 88" wide may be pieced in horizontal pieces as shown in Figure 12.

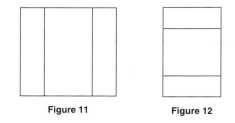

Figure 11   Figure 12

Layering the Quilt Sandwich

Layering the quilt top with the batting and backing is time-consuming. Open the batting several days before you need it and place over a bed or flat on the floor to help flatten the creases caused from folds.

Iron the backing piece, folding in half both vertically and horizontally, and pressing to mark the centers.

If you are quilting in a frame, place the backing in the frame, right side down. Place the batting on the backing, smoothing out wrinkles. Trim batting to match backing. Pin quilt top right side up on batting, adjusting to be sure blocks are square.

If you are quilting in a hoop, place the ironed backing right side down on a clean floor or table. Place the batting on top of the backing, smoothing out any wrinkles. Trim the batting to the same size as the backing. Place the quilt top on top of the batting, wrong side against the batting. Working from the center to the outside edges, smooth out any wrinkles or lumps.

To hold the quilt layers together for quilting, baste by hand or use safety pins. If basting by hand, thread a long thin needle with a long piece of unknotted white or off-white thread. Starting in the center and leaving a long tail, make 4"–6"-long stitches toward the outside edge of the quilt top, smoothing as you baste. Start at the center again and work toward the outside as shown in Figure 13.

Figure 13

If quilting by machine, you may prefer to use safety pins to hold your fabric sandwich together. Follow instructions for quilting in a hoop, substituting pins for needle and thread. To use pins, start in the center of the quilt and pin to the outside, leaving pins open until all are placed. When you are satisfied that all layers are smooth, close the pins. To use basting spray, follow the manufacturer's instructions on the container.

QUILTING

Hand Quilting

Hand quilting is the process of placing stitches through the quilt top, batting and backing to hold them together. While it serves a functional purpose, it also adds beauty and loft to the finished quilt.

To begin, thread a sharp between needle with an 18" piece of quilting thread. Tie a small knot in the end of the thread. Position the needle about ½"–1" away from the starting point on the quilt top. Sink needle through the top into the batting layer but not through the backing. Pull the needle up at the starting point of the quilting design. Pull the needle and thread until the knot sinks through the top into the batting (Figure 14).

Take small, even running stitches along the marked quilting line (Figure 15). Keep one hand po-

| Figure 14 | Figure 15 |

sitioned underneath to feel the needle go all the way through to the backing.

When you have nearly run out of thread, wind the thread around the needle several times to make a small knot and pull it close to the fabric. Insert the needle into the fabric on the quilting line and come out with the needle ½"–1" away, pulling the knot into the fabric layers the same as when you started. Pull and cut thread close to fabric. The end should disappear inside after cutting.

Machine Quilting

Successful machine quilting requires practice. Special machine-quilting needles work best to penetrate the three layers in your quilt.

Prepare the quilt for machine quilting in the same way as for hand quilting. Use safety pins to hold the layers together instead of basting with thread.

Presser-foot quilting is best used for straight-line quilting because the presser bar lever does not need to be continually lifted. Set the machine on a longer stitch length (3.0 or 8–10 stitches to the inch). Too tight a stitch causes puckering and fabric tucks, either

on the quilt top or backing. An even-feed or walking foot helps to eliminate the tucks and puckering by feeding the upper and lower layers through the machine evenly. Before you begin, loosen the amount of pressure on the presser foot.

For free-motion quilting, use your machine's darning foot with the feed dogs down. Refer to your sewing machine manual for other special instructions. Practice on a sample before trying this method on your quilt.

FINISHING THE EDGES

After your quilt is quilted, the edges need to be finished, but you must decide how you want the edges of your quilt finished before layering the backing and batting with the quilt top.

Without Binding—Self-Finish

There are several ways to eliminate adding an edge finish. This is done before quilting.

Method 1: Create a pocket

1. Place the batting on a flat surface.

2. Place the pieced top right side up on the batting.

3. Place the backing right sides together with the pieced top.

4. Pin and/or baste the layers together to hold flat referring to Layering the Quilt Sandwich.

5. Begin stitching in the center of one side using a ¼" seam allowance, reversing at the beginning and end of the seam. Continue stitching all around and back to the beginning side. Leave a 12" or larger opening. Clip corners to reduce excess.

6. Turn right side out through the opening.

7. Turn the raw edges in ¼" and slipstitch the opening closed by hand. The quilt may now be quilted by hand or machine.

The disadvantage to this method is that once the edges are stitched, any creases or wrinkles that might form during the quilting process cannot be flattened out. Tying is the preferred method for finishing a quilt constructed using this method.

Method 2: Use the backing

Bringing the backing fabric to the front is another method of self-finishing.

1. Complete the quilt as for hand or machine quilting.

2. Trim only the batting even with the quilt top. Trim the backing 1" larger than the completed top all around.

3. Turn the backing edge ½" to the wrong side; fold to overlap onto the front of the quilt ¼".

4. Machine-stitch close to the edge through all layers, or blind-stitch in place to finish.

Method 3: Use the top

The front may be turned to the back. If using this method, a wider front border is needed.

1. Trim the backing and batting 1" smaller than the top.

2. Turn the top edge under ½" and then turn to the back.

3. Stitch in place.

Method 4: Stitch top and back together

The top and backing may be stitched together by hand at the edge. To accomplish this, quilting must be stopped ½" from the quilt-top edge.

1. Trim the top and backing even and trim the batting to ¼"–½" smaller.

2. Turn under the edges of the top and backing ¼"–½".

3. Blind-stitch top and backing together at the very edge.

These methods do not require the use of extra fabric and save time in preparation of binding strips; they are not as durable as an added binding.

Binding

The technique of adding extra fabric at the edges of the quilt is called binding. The binding encloses the edges and adds an extra layer of fabric for durability. The instructions given with most of the projects in this book list cutting for a number of 2¼"-wide binding strips. Use these strips and follow the instructions for double-fold, straight-grain binding.

To prepare a quilt for the addition of the binding, trim the batting and backing layers even with the top of the quilt using a rotary cutter and ruler, or shears. Using a walking-foot attachment (sometimes called an even-feed foot attachment), machine-baste the three layers together all around approximately ⅛" from the cut edge.

Bias binding may be purchased in packages in many different colors but is not always available in a color to match your quilt. The advantage to self-made binding is that you can use fabrics from your quilt to coordinate colors.

Double-fold, straight-grain binding and double-fold, bias-grain binding are two of the most commonly used types of binding.

Double-fold, straight-grain binding is commonly used on the edges of quilts with square corners. Double-fold, bias-grain binding is best suited for quilts with rounded corners or scalloped edges.

Straight-Grain Binding

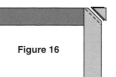

Figure 16

To make double-fold, straight-grain binding, cut 2¼"-wide strips of fabric across the width or down the length of the fabric totaling the perimeter of the quilt plus 12". The strips are joined as shown in Figure 16 and pressed in half wrong sides together along the length using an iron on a cotton setting with no steam.

Applying Binding Using Mitered Corners

1. Lining up the raw edges, place the binding on the

top of the quilt and begin sewing (again using the walking foot) approximately 6" from the beginning of the binding strip. Stop sewing ¼" from the first corner, leave the needle in the quilt, turn and sew diagonally to the corner as shown in Figure 17.

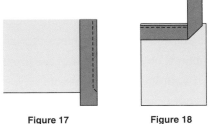

Figure 17   Figure 18

2. Fold the binding at a 45-degree angle up and away from the quilt as shown in Figure 18 and back down even with the raw edge of the next side of the quilt.

3. Starting at the top raw edge of the quilt, begin sewing the next side as shown in Figure 19. Repeat at the next three corners.

Figure 19

4. As you approach the beginning of the binding strip, stop stitching and overlap the binding ends ½"; trim. Join the two ends with a ¼" seam allowance and press the seam open.

5. Reposition the joined binding along the edge of the quilt and resume stitching to the beginning.

6. To finish, bring the folded edge of the binding over the raw edges and blind-stitch the binding in place over the machine-stitching line on the back side. Hand-miter the corners on the back as shown in Figure 20.

Figure 20

Note: Another option when you approach the beginning of the binding strip is to stop stitching and lay the end across the beginning so it will slip inside the fold. Cut the end at a 45-degree angle so the raw edges are contained inside the beginning of the strip (Figure 21). Resume stitching to the beginning. Bring the fold to the back of the quilt and hand-stitch as previously described.

Figure 21

Applying Binding Using Overlapped Corners

Overlapped corners are easier than mitered corners.

1. Sew binding strips to opposite sides of the quilt top.

2. Turn the folded edge to the back side and stitch edges down to finish.

3. Trim ends even.

4. Sew a strip to each remaining side, leaving 1½"–2" excess at each end.

5. Turn quilt over and fold binding end in even with previous finished edge as shown in Figure 22.

Figure 22   Figure 23

6. Fold binding over onto quilt back and stitch down as before, enclosing the previous bound edge in the seam as shown in Figure 23. It may be necessary to trim the folded-down section to reduce bulk.

Bias-Grain Binding

When you are using bias-grain binding, you have the option to eliminate the corners if it doesn't interfere with the patchwork in the quilt. Round the corners off by placing a dinner plate

Figure 24

at the corner and rotary-cutting the gentle curve (Figure 24).

Making Bias-Grain Binding

1. To make double-fold, bias-grain binding, cut 2¼"-wide bias strips from the binding-fabric yardage.

2. Join the strips as shown in Figure 25 and press seams open.

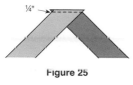

Figure 25

3. Fold the joined strips in half with wrong sides together along the length, and press with no steam as for straight-grain binding.

Follow the same procedures as previously described for sewing the binding to the quilt top.

Making Continuous Bias Binding

Instead of cutting individual bias strips and sewing them together, you may make continuous bias binding.

1. Cut a square 18" x 18" from chosen binding fabric.

2. Cut the square in half on one diagonal to make two triangles as shown in Figure 26.

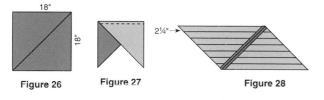

Figure 26   Figure 27   Figure 28

3. With right sides together, join the two triangles with a ¼" seam allowance as shown in Figure 27; press seam open to reduce bulk.

4. Mark lines every 2¼" on the wrong side of the fabric as shown in Figure 28.

5. Bring the short ends right sides together, offsetting one line as shown in Figure 29; stitch to make a tube. This will seem awkward.

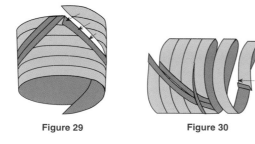

Figure 29   Figure 30

6. Begin cutting at point A as shown in Figure 30; continue cutting along marked line to make one continuous strip.

7. Fold strip in half along length with wrong sides together; press.

Follow the same procedures as previously described for sewing on the binding.

FINAL TOUCHES

If your quilt will be hung on the wall, a hanging sleeve is needed; a fabric sleeve will evenly distribute the weight of the quilt across the top edge.

Adding a Sleeve

1. Measure across the top of the finished quilt.

2. Cut an 8"-wide piece of muslin equal to that length—you may need to join several muslin strips to make the required length.

3. Fold in ¼" on each end of the muslin strip and press. Fold again and stitch to hold.

4. Fold the muslin strip with right sides together along the length. Sew along the long side to make a tube.

5. Turn the tube right side out; press with seam at bottom or centered on the back.

6. Hand-stitch the top of the tube along the top of the quilt and the bottom of the tube to the quilt back, making sure the quilt lies flat. Stitches should not go through to the front of the quilt and don't need to be too close together.

7. Slip a wooden dowel or long curtain rod through the sleeve to hang.

Dating the Quilt

When the quilt is complete, it should be signed and dated. Use a permanent pen on the back of the quilt. Other methods include cross-stitching your name and date on the front or back, or making a permanent label that may be stitched to the back.

SPECIAL THANKS

We would like to thank the talented quilt designers whose work is featured in this collection.

Mary Ayres
Dainty Handkerchief, 96
Fancy Needlework Basket, 25

Karen Blocher
20/20 Spring Fling, 71

Barbara A. Clayton
All-Sports Growth Chart, 33
Christmas Holly Place Mat, 154
Rooster Wall Quilt, 56
Sunflower Table Runner, 64
Trailing Ivy Roll Cover, 38
Trailing Ivy Tissue Box Cover, 41

Holly Daniels
Fourth of July Picnic Blanket, 122

Sue Harvey & Sandy Boobar
Stained Glass Circles, 60

Sandra L. Hatch
Blooming Flowers, 74
Cookie-Cutter Crazy, 86
Merry Christmas Bag, 145

Connie Kauffman
The Scent of Lilacs, 10
Springtime Table Mat, 116

Chris Malone
Beaded Patchwork
    Ornaments, 157
Patchwork Posies, 90

Rochelle Martin
Happy Days, 131

Doris Nowell
Pretty in Pink, 50

Connie Rand
Happy Snowmen
    Place Mat, 148
Field of Sunflowers, 125

Jill Reber
Ducks in a Row, 53
Posie Party, 47
Shimmering Snowflakes, 162
Square Dance, 134

Nancy Richoux
Ladybug Runner, 67
Quilted Fridge Frames, 28

Judith Sandstrom
Fancy Bars, 13

Marinda Stewart
A Touch of Elegance, 99

Ruth Swasey
Four-Square Fantasy, 140

Jodi G. Warner
Toy Boat Regatta, 78

Julie Weaver
Picture This, 128
Table Grace, 119
Twinkle, Twinkle
    Christmas Stars, 167

Johanna Wilson
Red, White & Blue
    Americana, 22
Scrappy Four-Patch, 19
Strips & Stripes, 137

Janet Jones Worley
Almost Amish Scrap Quilt, 16

FABRICS & SUPPLIES

Page 10: The Scent of Lilacs—Heirloom Lilac fabric collection from RJR Fashion Fabrics and Blendable and Cotton threads from Sulky.

Page 47: Posie Party—Master Piece 45 ruler and Static Stickers from Master Piece Products and Presencia thread and pearl cotton.

Page 53: Ducks in a Row—Master Piece 45 ruler and Static Stickers from Master Piece Products and Presencia thread and pearl cotton.

Page 74: Blooming Flowers—Over the Rainbow fabric collection from Robert Kaufman, White Rose cotton batting from Mountain Mist, Star Machine Quilting Thread from Coats, Accu-Cut flower die No. 14 and GrandeMark die-cutting machine. Stitched on an InnovisD from Brother International. Machine-quilted by Dianne Hodgkins.

Page 86: Cookie-Cutter Crazy—The Warmth of Christmas fabric collection from Northcott, Star Multicolor Machine Quilting Thread from Coats and Cotton Classic batting from Fairfield Processing. Machine-quilted by Lorraine Sweet.

Page 99: A Touch of Elegance—A Touch of Elegance fabric collection from RJR Fabrics and Cotton Classic batting and Soft Touch pillow forms from Fairfield Processing.

Page 116: Springtime Table Mat—Hobbs Heirloom fusible batting and Sulky variegated and cotton threads.

Page 125: Field of Sunflowers—Machine 60/40 Blend batting from Fairfield Processing and Star Machine Quilting Thread from Coats.

Page 128: Picture This—Hobbs Thermore Batting.

Page 131: Happy Days—Fabrics from Timeless Treasures, Machine 60/40 Blend batting from Fairfield Processing and Star Machine Quilting Thread from Coats.

Page 134: Square Dance—Master Piece 45 ruler and Static Stickers from Master Piece Products and Presencia thread and pearl cotton.

Page 162: Shimmering Snowflakes—Master Piece 45 ruler and Static Stickers from Master Piece Products and Presencia thread and pearl cotton.